How do I increase my CQ?

What are cultural values?

Why should I confront
my hidden biases?

How do I move
beyond tolerance?

EXPLORING CQ

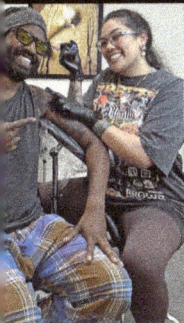

What People are saying about Exploring CQ

"Wilbur has created a masterpiece! Embracing well-researched scientific material, and peppered extensively with stories of his boundless, intriguing adventures and experiences, this book reveals for us the sheer exotic diversity of humans thriving on our planet Earth. I love the book! It epitomizes Wilbur as an artist, an actor, a musician, and an author with an empathic educator ethos."

Professor Soon Ang (PhD),
Nanyang Business School, Distinguished University Professor
Founder and Executive Director, Center for Leadership & Cultural
Intelligence, Singapore

"Completely fresh, Wilbur Sargunaraj's book will pique your curiosity, make you laugh, and teach you valuable skills for working across cultures. Many try to write about culture in a way that is both fun and practical, but few succeed as Wilbur has in his book *Exploring CQ*. I highly recommend it!"

Erin Meyer, Author of *The Culture Map*
Professor of Management Practice, INSEAD, Paris, France

"With so much hatred and misunderstanding in the world, Wilbur offers something different – hope. He does this not by pretending to know all the answers, but by being human and bringing readers with him as he journeys around the world, making plenty of mistakes along the way. A heartwarming, instructive and highly readable book every human should keep in their toolbox."

Katya Cengel, Journalist and Author of *Exiled*
Lecturer at Journalism Department,
Cal- Poly, San Luis Obispo, United States

"In *Exploring CQ*, Wilbur shares profound insights and guides readers on a transformative journey toward cultural intelligence and reconciliation. With humility and grace, Wilbur provides practical solutions, illuminating a path towards living in harmony among diverse cultures. Drawing from rich stories, Wilbur invites readers to embrace a new paradigm - one that honours Whanaungatanga (interconnectedness) of all people, and fosters genuine reconciliation. This is an important book which is certain to empower and transform people here in Aotearoa, New Zealand and all around the world. Whether you are Indigenous, settler, Pakeha or Māori, and wherever you are from, this book will help you relate to your fellow humans with love, respect, empathy and understanding. I love Wilbur's message and urge you to read *Exploring CQ.*"

Dr. Pouroto Ngaropō, Tohunga, Historian, Senior Cultural Advisor
Iramoko Marae, Aotearoa, New Zealand

"In the traditional hero's journey, the hero sets out to capture or control something. Wilbur's journeys, by contrast, start from wonder and a desire to learn. That openness is the lesson of cultural intelligence—in our embrace of the ways of others we come to understand a kernel of our shared humanity—coping, struggling, and celebrating TOGETHER. This book will leave a lasting impression on you."

Dr. Ronald D. Lalonde, Founding Director
River's Path Professional Coaching, Saudi Arabia

"Our work with reconciliation involves bringing Indigenous, non-Indigenous and newcomers together, yet people often wonder how to make this a tangible reality. This beautiful book can help people to take practical steps towards reconciliation using cultural intelligence and show them ways to overcome the biases and stereotypes that keep us all apart. I highly recommend this book to all those who are interested in exploring ways to develop cross-cultural relationships and work towards genuine reconciliACTION."

Mary Musqua-Culbertson, Treaty Commissioner of Saskatchewan
Treaty 6 Territory, Turtle Island, Canada

"*Exploring CQ* tells a story of self-discovery and how Wilbur methodically built the skills to befriend anyone from anywhere in the world - because what makes someone culturally intelligent is not the number of countries traveled, but the number of friends made along the way. And by this standard, Wilbur is a CQ master! He draws from personal experience and provides heartwarming anecdotes to guide readers through the intricacies of connecting with diverse cultures. This book will empower you to embark on a remarkable journey of friendship and understanding, and is for anyone who believes in the power of human connection."

Dr. Catherine Wu, Lecturer
Leadership, Management, & Organizations,
Nanyang Business School, Singapore

"After reading *Exploring CQ* I was left with a feeling of hope. Wilbur's message is universal. I believe that deep down we all want to build relationships and overcome bias, but the 'how' seems daunting. This book will give you simple and practical steps to begin this journey. Apart from sharing this book with the public, I am excited to share it with my children so together we can learn how to better exercise cultural intelligence. If our youngest generation has guidance from the beginning on how to be culturally respectful and build good relationships, what a wonderful world this will be! I urge you to grab a copy of *Exploring CQ!*"

Tammy Willman, Program Director, Grand Coteau Heritage and Cultural Centre, Shaunavon, Saskatchewan, Treaty 6 Territory, Canada

"I met Wilbur years ago, in preparation for his journey to Rwanda. He wanted to learn how Rwandans were recovering from the 1994 genocide against the Tutsi, when more than one million people were killed. I had been working there during those brutal 100 days of slaughter. As we spoke together, I got my first glimpse into his deep passion for building bridges of connection and understanding over and around the multitude of misconceptions dividing our beautiful globe! I've enjoyed many visits and conversations with Wilbur since that day. This book felt like a beautiful continuation of those conversations. Wilbur skillfully weaves research together with real life experiences to create an entertaining and insightful journey into cultural intelligence. My heart was touched and my mind challenged on page after page as Wilbur, with wisdom and considerable vulnerability, took me from country to country on a wonderful journey! I loved the joyful and often poignant video clip links generously scattered through the book. It's story-based-learning at its best!"

Carl Wilkens, Author of *I'm Not Leaving*
Co-founder and Director, World Outside My Shoes,
Spokane, United States

"*Exploring CQ* is a valuable resource that will help deepen people's understanding of how to enhance cross-cultural exchanges and relationships. This accessible book contains practical applications for anyone who reads it. With increasingly diverse schools, this book is particularly beneficial for educators and newcomers. Wilbur's real-life stories cause the reader to laugh, relate, learn, and be inspired all at the same time. I am truly excited for how this book can build understanding and create a more beautiful world!"

LeeAnne Benjamin, English as an Additional Language Teacher, M.Ed.
Saskatoon, Saskatchewan, Treaty 6 Territory, Canada

Cover and interior design by PrintPro | www.printprowinnipeg.com
Additional graphic design: Anna Muthu Diederichs

Cover Photo by Claire House Photography
Hongi with Dr. Pouroto Ngaropō

ISBN 978-1-9994465-1-2

EXPLORING CQ

Building Relationships using Cultural Intelligence

WILBUR SARGUNARAJ

To my Amma, who taught me above all how to love and develop meaningful relationships.

Photo: Alexis Pimentel

Exploring CQ was written on Treaty 6 territory, the homeland of many First Nations and the Métis people on Turtle Island (Canada). It is my hope that this book will inspire all people to work towards genuine reconciliation while building bridges across cultures.

CONTENTS

FOREWORD

While political leaders argue about the pros and cons of multiculturalism, wokeness, and diversity, the rest of us are going about our everyday lives in neighbourhoods, towns, and countries that are increasingly characterized by people from a diversity of backgrounds. We don't all have to eat the same things, celebrate the same holidays, or even believe the same things. But we do have to figure out how to get along. Just about the time that the task of getting along feels increasingly difficult, along comes the world-renowned performer, thought leader, and Simple Superstar Wilbur Sargunaraj to help us do more than just get along. He shows us how to open up our hearts and minds to discover our shared humanity by exploring our differences and celebrating them. I've spent the last 25 years working with my colleague Soon Ang to study cultural intelligence—the capability to work and relate with people from different cultural backgrounds. Or more simply—the ability to get along with anyone, anywhere. Soon and I have always agreed that our work in cultural intelligence is meaningless unless it's translated into stories and practical advice that all of us can use. That's why I love Wilbur's work. He draws upon our research together with his global travels, his multicultural upbringing, and his creative genius to write songs, create exhibitions, and now to write a book that tells us in simple yet profound language how cultural intelligence can help all of us. You're about to embark on a journey around the world that in typical Wilbur style includes humour, insight, riveting stories, and provocative challenges for using cultural intelligence to improve the way we interact with our neighbours next door and around the world. I hope you enjoy *Exploring CQ* as much as I did.

David Livermore, Founder of the Cultural Intelligence Centre, PhD, Boston University

PREFACE

The Eastern Latrine

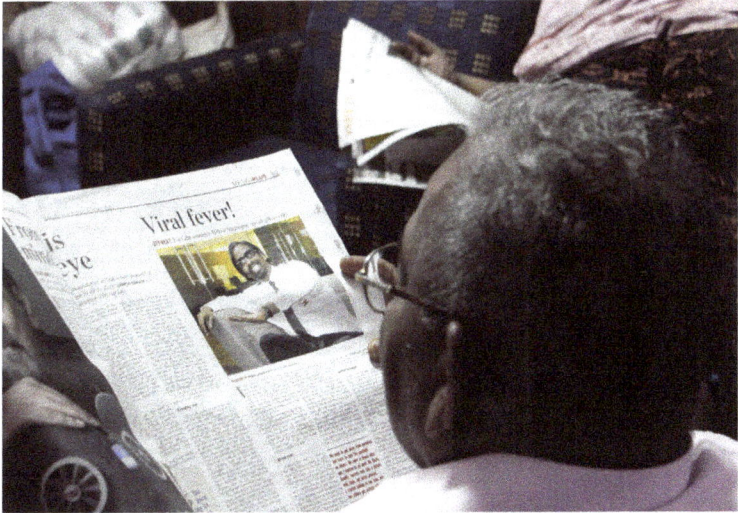

I still remember the day when my friend called me up and said, "Wilbur, you've gone viral." At that time, the only association I had with that word was sickness!

"What do you mean, I went viral?" I asked.

"Your toilet video is all over the internet," my friend replied, with unbridled excitement.

YouTube was in its infancy, and I had just uploaded one of my first instructional videos, a tutorial explaining how to use an Indian toilet. It wasn't a slick video with high production values; it was raw, and filmed in standard definition. I convinced my sister to be the videographer, and we used the outdoor toilets at our village home in Virudhunagar District, Tamil Nadu.

Looking back, I don't know why I made this particular video. I wasn't passionate about toilets, but for a long time I felt that someone needed to be clear and explain some of the customs that are part of using an eastern latrine! Squatting, aiming for the hole, using hands to clean, the bucket and dipper are all part of the experience!

I found the comment section under the video quite entertaining. Some Indians were mad that I was showcasing an Asian squat toilet in so much detail, while others loved the humorous and direct approach. Some people from outside India were thankful that I had gone to great lengths to show what to do when you don't have toilet paper, while others were downright disgusted!

I realized that this was a fabulous way to help people understand similarities and differences between cultures, and so began the toilet tutorials. Every time I went overseas for work, I decided to film a video. How does one use a Balinese eco-toilet that uses woodchips to flush? How do you balance on two planks in a Mongolian rural toilet? What about the African pit latrine in Uganda where you use leaves or newspapers instead of toilet paper, or the Japanese washlet where you are serenaded by sounds to cover your noisy 'business'?

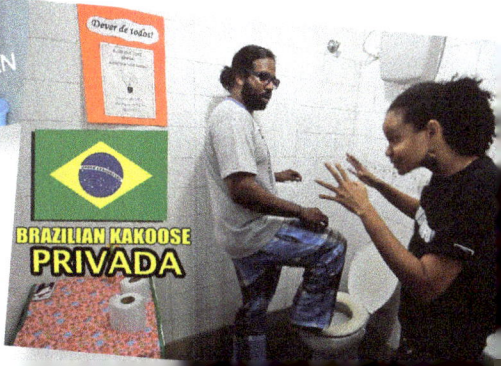

ENJOY THE WATER BUTTOX MASSAGE!

BUANG AIR BESAR
Indonesian word for kaka!

DO NOT USE HAND TO CLEAN WITHOUT THE WATER!!!

Dever de todos!

BRAZILIAN KAKOOSE
PRIVADA

화장실 Hwajangsil

Do not squat on one plank!

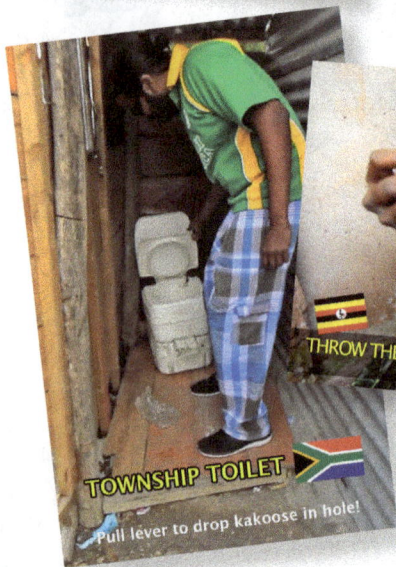

TOWNSHIP TOILET

Pull lever to drop kakoose in hole!

THROW THE USED LEAF IN THE HOLE!

The Times of India even decided to do a feature write up, and I'm still not sure what I thought about that! Were my parents supposed to be proud? Instead of making it on to MTV or becoming a doctor, software engineer or lawyer, their son was in the news for showing people how to use toilets!

This is when I decided to start on a new video series called First Class Eats. Why stop at toilets when you can make educational videos about the very thing that sends you to the toilet? Eating insects in Cambodia, sheep's head in Norway, the buttocks of ants in Colombia – I discovered that there was even more interest regarding exotic foods than there was for toilets, and that these videos created space for discussion.

Talking about food and toilets makes the playing field level for all humans. We all need to eat, and we all need to relieve ourselves – and I found that people were most engaged by these two topics when it came to learning about different cultures. Armed with a new tool I was on a mission – not only to help people learn about unique foods and remote toilets, but to help them navigate cross-cultural relationships. All of this began with an eastern latrine in Tamil Nadu.

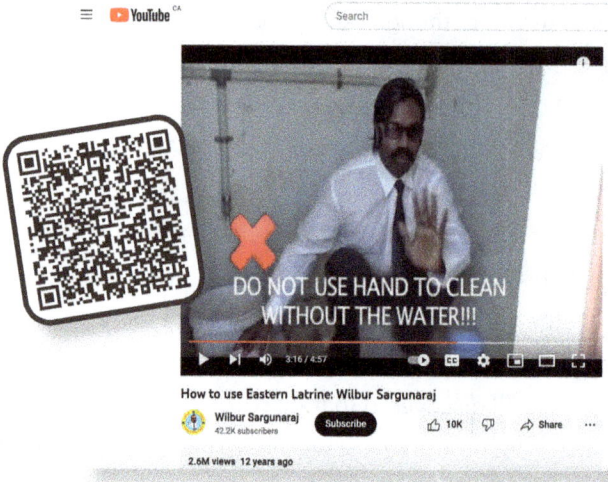

This book is the culmination of a lifetime of cross-cultural interactions and experiences. Whether living in Tamil Nadu or Tokyo, villages in South Asia or small towns in Saskatchewan, cultural intelligence (CQ) has been an integral part of my journey in developing relationships around the world – before I even knew what it was. This book is about how to effectively interact with people from different cultures using the power of CQ.

I was introduced to the term CQ by the Cultural Intelligence Centre. (Yes! There is an actual academic centre devoted to researching CQ!) After releasing a number of music videos and short films about various cultures, I started receiving messages from educators, saying that my content was being used in their colleges, high schools, and universities to teach students about cultural differences. It was around this time that I was introduced to two academics and authorities on cultural intelligence: Professor Soon Ang from the Nanyang Technological University in Singapore, and Dr. David Livermore from the CQ Centre in Michigan, USA. They were curious about the content I was releasing, which would often show me developing relationships while moving in and out of numerous cultural contexts. I was equally curious and fascinated to discover that my cultural intelligence could be assessed; and it was at this point that I was able to name cultural intelligence, understand the framework for thinking about it, and analyze the actual strategies I was using when making cross-cultural connections.

I received certification as a Cultural Intelligence Facilitator through the CQ Centre, and used that knowledge in my role as an educator and performing artist. My work has taken me into organisations varying from academic institutions to corporate conferences, and in all of them I get to share practical solutions, through music and workshops, on how to build bridges across cultures.

Inspired by the research that has been conducted about cultural values, I also decided to create an educational exhibition where people are introduced to cultural intelligence and could learn about it at their own pace. I would share stories at gallery events which were not part of the display itself, and this led to numerous requests for a book to go along with the exhibition. Since the format of a photography exhibition also made it hard to share in-depth stories and experiences that were an integral part of my cultural intelligence education, I wanted to create something which people could take away from my events and exhibitions, something to help them remember what they had just experienced.

This is when the *Exploring CQ* book was born. The goal of this book is to help everyone to gain a better understanding of cultural intelligence, so they can be more effective in their interactions with people from different cultures.

In *Exploring CQ* we'll start our journey with an introduction to who I am, and some of my first experiences of encountering people from different cultures and backgrounds. We will then look at the four capabilities of cultural intelligence. The cultural values, and the cultural clusters that have been developed by researchers in the field of cultural intelligence will also be explored. At the end of the book, I share thoughts on unconscious bias, fear of the 'other' (those not like us), and how CQ can be used in reconciliation.

Throughout this book I will share stories so you can practically see how I used CQ to develop relationships. Stories are easy to remember and are a powerful tool for learning. Peppered

through the book you will see photographs as well as thumbnails of various YouTube videos from my cultural intelligence channel that go along with these stories. Scan the QR code and watch these fun and informative videos!

This book is based around the idea that CQ can be used for much more than just knowledge on how to interact effectively across cultures. CQ can be used to build relationships. When using the word, 'relationship' I mean the development of personal connections that result when one moves towards another person, seeking to understand them and their values, as opposed to retreating behind walls based on difference. It is my hope that as you learn about cultural intelligence, you will come to realize its potential in revealing our common humanity and how it can be used to truly make our world more whole.

Thanks for exploring CQ with me!

Wilbur Sargunaraj,
Treaty 6 Territory, Canada

INTRODUCTION

The Tamil Mennonite who speaks Japanese - A mini autobiography

I was born in a small town in Canada, to very traditional Tamil parents who were extremely patriotic Indians. Tamil Nadu is located at the southern tip of India and is considered the cultural and linguistic mecca for Tamils. Tamil people also place significance on auspicious dates so it's worth mentioning that I was born on 7/7/77. (The Seventh Day Adventist school I attended for a year; initially thought I was the chosen one but their opinion quickly changed!) My parents moved to Canada as my Appa (dad) wanted to receive theological training to become a pastor. Being patriotic Indians and not too fond of the bitter cold, as soon as my dad completed his studies, we moved back to hot and sunny India.

I was given the name Wilbur by my Thatha (grandfather), who convinced my parents to name me after his close friend Hoffermayer Wilbur, who was his overseas pen-pal. My patriotic Amma was mortified! A German name for her Tamil son? She quickly shot down the idea of 'Hoffermayer' and settled for 'Wilbur', then honoured my thatha by giving me his name: 'Sargunaraj'. While I'm glad the name Hoffermayer didn't stick, every now and then I can't help but daydream about the spectacular stage name I might have had if I transformed my amateur yodelling talents into a professional career!

My Thatha, Mr. Sargunaraj

Yodeling in the Swiss Alps

From a young age I remember being fascinated by countries. I loved quizzing myself about colourful flags, capitals of the world, and commercial airplane liveries. Geography was my favourite subject, and I developed a burning curiosity about the differences and similarities between people from these countries.

At first I thought the world was one big happy family, and that we could all come together by being nice and sporting big smiles. Having a dad who was a preacher meant my parents moved around a lot, so I was constantly being introduced to new cultures, and had to adapt quickly.

I realized that even though people could be nice, they often harbored biases and were fearful of differences. I noticed that it was much easier to stay within your group, with people who looked like you and shared similar beliefs and value systems. These experiences made me reflect about my identity and learn to appreciate differences when meeting people from various cultures.

I spent a year of my childhood at international schools in the hill stations of Darjeeling and Udhagamandalam (also known as Ooty or 'Queen of Hill Stations') while my parents were busy setting up medical clinics in rural India. This is where British and Australian classmates gave me my first introduction to cultural differences. I was teased for being a brown-skinned Indian who ate curry and in turn, I would tease them for being pasty white like 'skimmed milk' and for eating abominable things like Marmite and Vegemite! (If you aren't familiar with these foods, they are salty dark brown pastes made from yeast extract and by-products of beer making!) Doesn't that sound appetizing? After my introduction to these strange foods and cultures, my family relocated to the cities of Varanasi and Calcutta where I had to eat more strange food, and where Hindi was the dominant language.

Being a Tamil in North India had its challenges. Moving from state to state within India is like moving between different countries. The language, attire, and customs are all completely different, giving you a feeling that you are a foreigner in your own country. At home I spoke Tamil with my parents, I studied in an English medium school, and I learned Hindi as a second language.

My parents then decided they wanted to be close to their families, so we finally ended up in my home state of Tamil Nadu. It was here that I made friends with Hindus, Muslims, Jains, and Sikhs – and the wonderful sport of cricket is what brought us all together! I felt comfortable there; while we all had different religious backgrounds, we all spoke Tamil, and we were all from Tamil Nadu. While by birth I was marked as a Canadian on documents, I grew up in India as a proper Tamil boy. Dad was from a small village and mom was from the city, so we lived in two worlds, interacting with people from both the village and the city. After a while, the pressure from traditional Indian society that I should become a doctor, lawyer, or software engineer began to catch up with me (not to mention the pressure to follow my dad's footsteps and be a pastor)! Knowing that I couldn't pursue a career as an artist in Tamil Nadu, I begged my parents to send me to Canada.

During my teenage years I left for the place of my birth and ended up in a small Mennonite German village on Treaty 6 Territory in the province of Saskatchewan, Canada, where my parents had several friends. This was not the multicultural or diverse Canada that we all hear about now. Back in the day I was the only dark-skinned person in a sea of Caucasian Mennonites!

Wait! That's not entirely true! There were other 'Indians'. I never encountered the Indigenous people of Treaty 6 Territory. They lived far away on designated areas called reservations, or in the cities. Because I lived in a small isolated community, I never really saw them. I'll admit that even though I loved learning about cultures, I was quite ignorant, and my knowledge about the First Nations in Canada was limited. My idea of this country was that it was formed and founded by peaceful Mennonite farmers!

Wilbur from India was welcomed and treated well for the most part. I think there was a sense of curiosity about who I was, and because I had good spoken English (albeit with an accent), and because I assimilated quickly into the local culture, I was accepted. I found out that the 'other Indians' were not treated so well. There was an unspoken fear of the First Nations, and hurtful stereotypes ran rampant, many of which I learned and internalized.

I never made friends with any First Nations people during this time, and I wasn't taught Indigenous history in school. In fact, I found out later that while I was still in school, the last residential school for Indigenous people in Canada was still in operation, and it was just a short drive from where I lived. These institutions were set up for cultural genocide and assimilation and were only shut down around the time I graduated. As I grew older, I confronted my own bias, which led me down a path of reconciliation and allowed me to develop friendships with Indigenous people across the country.

After three years of being immersed in this rural farming community you could say I became part Mennonite. I could drop some Plautdietsch (low-German) when I needed to, and I felt quite comfortable eating kieleke (noodles) and shmonfat (gravy). After growing up in India where marriages were arranged, I was now introduced to the concept of dating. The parents of the Mennonite girl I was interested in weren't fully convinced about their future grandchildren being of a mixed race, so this ended quickly in heartbreak. This was another time I realized I was 'different'.

Being dark-skinned in a small prairie village does have its perks though. Many people in the community thought I was black, so I went along with it. There was a strong association that being black meant you were cool, and so as a teenager struggling with my identity, I told everyone my great grandparents were African, got a flattop haircut, ditched cricket and took up basketball. "Yo! They got a black guy on their team!" I would hear. I was Wilbur, the Menno-Tamil wannabe-African boy who couldn't play basketball, but would strike terror into the hearts of rural Canadian high school basketball teams! My dreams of being in the NBA ended early, but I continued to pursue my childhood dream of being a musician.

After graduating from music college I started touring professionally, and work took me to various countries where I continued to enjoy developing new friendships and getting to know different perspectives.

Identity crisis: The Flattop!

I lived in Japan for a year, and was a drummer for a rock band that included members from Italy, Germany, France, Spain, and England. We immersed ourselves in the fascinating culture of Japan, and of course we got to know each other's quirky and diverse cultures as we rocked out in the clubs of Roppongi every weekend. This was one of the times when I came to know that creating long-lasting and genuine friendships with people from different cultures was possible. By the time I left the country, I was fluent in conversational Japanese, and I'm proud to say it was far better than my low German!

I continued to collaborate with local musicians in different countries, creating songs that would combine various languages and musical styles. Music videos like *Boda Boda*, *Bunny Chow*, and *Simple Súperstarella* were all written to help people catch glimpses of different cultures.

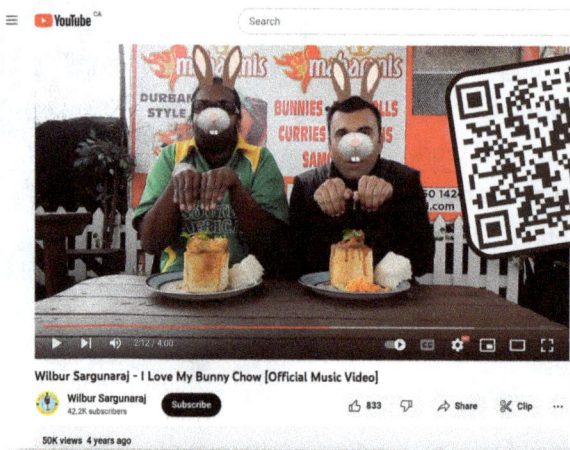

While my time in the Mennonite community and in Japan was mostly positive, my first experience of encountering overt bias was during a music tour in China. I was part of a thirteen-city tour and was just learning how to drink tea without milk and sugar. I was also getting used to eating snake, horse, cow stomach, and myriad other dishes that would have shocked my mom. While the people I met were quite friendly, I noticed something strange. My picture was never used in any of the publicity or promotional material. Our Chinese tour manager would always make sure our event was publicized in the local media, and at each city I would open a paper with surprise. All my Caucasian band mates were featured, and for some reason my photo never made it to press! While I didn't let it bother me, I started wondering whether my photo would have made it if I were white-skinned.

I remember even the rest of the team started noticing this. The most interesting incident was in Guangzhou, where the local paper featured a huge spread featuring all ten of my bandmates, and instead of me on the drums there was a photoshopped picture of Paul McCartney playing with the band!

All these experiences opened my eyes to ways in which we put up walls, create barriers, perpetuate bias, and remain fearful of those who are different than ourselves. I knew that I could choose to stay with people who are similar to me, or I could take a risk and enrich myself with new experiences and make friends with Mennonites, Japanese, Chinese, First Nations, and even Australians who eat abominable Vegemite and call me brownie or curry-face!

Not everyone may undergo such experiences, but I am convinced that you don't have to travel to make deeper and more meaningful connections across cultures. With globalization and migration on the rise, there are countless opportunities to strengthen your cultural intelligence and build relationships without having to step on an airplane bound to a far-off country.

At my workshops in schools, kids frequently ask me how many countries I've visited – to which I always reply that it's not about how many countries I've visited, but about how many meaningful relationships I've been able to develop with people I've visited. That is what Exploring CQ is all about – making friends, and learning with people who are different than yourself.

CHAPTER 1

What Is CQ Anyway?

> *"Studying culture without experiencing culture shock is like practicing swimming without experiencing water."*
>
> ### Geert Hofstede

Cultural intelligence (CQ) is one of the research-based forms of intelligence, like IQ and EQ. Cultural intelligence stems from years of academic research and may sound complex, but it is quite easy to comprehend. In their book *Individual Interactions Across Cultures*, Soon Ang and Early Christopher state that **CQ is your ability to function and relate effectively with people from different cultures.** CQ provides a coherent framework to help people navigate cross-cultural interactions. While the fixed and innate nature of IQ is a subject of debate, the good news is that cultural intelligence is something that can always be developed!

THE FOUR CAPABILITIES OF CQ

Cultural intelligence rests on four capabilities. Understanding these capabilities can help you measure, enhance, and apply your CQ.

CQ Drive is your interest and motivation to function in diverse cultural situations.

CQ Knowledge is your understanding of how cultures are similar and different.

CQ Strategy is your awareness and ability to plan for multicultural interactions.

CQ Action is your ability to appropriately adjust behaviour in different cultural contexts.

I am sure that many of you reading this book have already been exercising these four capabilities without even realizing it! Let's say your neighbour or co-worker is from a different culture. CQ Drive is demonstrated when you eagerly initiate conversations with them. CQ Knowledge is exemplified when you take the time to learn about their culture. Now imagine they invite you to a special cultural event. CQ Strategy takes the form of strategically planning for the new encounter. When you adjust your speech, conversational style, or behaviour, this demonstrates that you are practising CQ Action. As you can see, the four capabilities of CQ present a straightforward and practical framework to help anyone interested in navigating the intricacies of cross-cultural relationships.

To exercise high cultural intelligence, a person does not need to be a globetrotter or a walking encyclopedia of cultural knowledge. Instead, a person with high CQ has a strong understanding of their own cultural identity, while being interested in getting to know the cultural identity of others. People with high CQ have a strong motivation to persevere through cross-cultural challenges and are able to navigate cultural differences. They are willing to examine their own biases and move beyond cultural stereotypes. They watch, listen, learn, and appropriately adjust their behaviour to form meaningful relationships with people from cultures other than their own. It's not just about being 'nice'! Many people can be culturally sensitive and 'nice' but still lack effectiveness in their interactions with people from other cultures. Regardless of where you live, how little or frequently you travel, you can increase your CQ by exercising these capabilities, knowing that cultural intelligence is an ongoing journey of personal growth and learning.

> **Cultural intelligence is your ability to function and relate effectively with people from different cultures.**

THE JAPANESE ONSEN

It was a muggy summer day in 2005 when I landed in Tokyo. I managed to navigate the friendly Japanese rail system and arrived at Yukarigaoka, a community nestled in the province of Chiba. I hadn't arrived here as a tourist, but had come to the country to work and get a better understanding of a culture that fascinated me. The day after I arrived in Japan, I decided to visit a swimming pool to seek relief from the sweltering heat.

While I had a general understanding of Japanese culture, I was certainly not aware of the meticulous protocols for bathing naked in an onsen (traditional hot springs)! I was told there was a clothed co-ed pool in the particular facility I visited, but with all the signage being in Japanese, I couldn't find it. I ended up in the area where people cleanse themselves before entering the onsen. Surrounded by naked men, I was even more desperate to find this elusive co-ed pool where people were clothed. Not knowing where to go and what to do, I sat in the farthest corner with my swimming trunks on and sheepishly tried to copy all the other men who were doing the customary cleansing.

Eventually I tip-toed to the onsen and entered with all eyes staring at me – and at my swimming trunks! A man who was visibly annoyed, got out and said something to me aggressively in Japanese which I didn't understand. The water was uncomfortably hot, but I didn't want to leave because it covered me up to my waist, and I felt embarrassed to make another mistake! Finally, a young Japanese teenager entered the onsen, looked at my shorts and said in a friendly voice, "Are you looking for the swimming pool?" With a huge sigh of relief, I followed him through the onsen until we reached the hidden pool! I turned towards the teenager and used the only word I knew at the time, "Arigato gozaimasu!" (thank you)!

I had experienced challenging cross-cultural situations in the past, but jumping into the Japanese onsen for the first time left me quite vulnerable. Looking back, I wish I would have known and exercised the four cultural intelligence capabilities to help me in this situation! Let's examine these capabilities through my experience at the Japanese onsen.

CQ DRIVE:

Am I interested in discovering or experiencing new cultural customs? Do I have the desire and perseverance to learn the cultural expectations needed for the Japanese onsen? Can I face my fears and bias?

CQ KNOWLEDGE:

Do I have an understanding of how the onsen is similar or different to swimming in my culture? Can I use my knowledge about the onsen to have a better experience? Can I put aside feelings of ethnocentricity (thinking my culture is better) because I believe my customs regarding public pools is better?

CQ STRATEGY:

Am I using my cultural knowledge to plan for this new cultural experience at the onsen? When I am at the onsen, can I check and test my own assumptions and plans by being aware and mindful of what is going on around me? Can I be flexible to change my plans in the moment as needed?

CQ ACTION:

Can I appropriately adjust my actions and behaviour in the onsen? Am I able to avoid cultural taboos? For example: not washing thoroughly before entering, or wearing swimming attire in the onsen are definitely taboo in Japan. Can I appropriately adjust my behaviour to enjoy this experience while staying true to myself?

Working on each of these four capabilities is a proven way to help you increase your cultural intelligence. Developing an interest, increasing your knowledge, asking questions, and adapting your behaviour are all part of the journey of becoming more culturally intelligent. While my onsen experience was mostly about cross-cultural etiquette, the next few stories focus on how I used the four capabilities of CQ to develop personal relationships across cultures.

THE FOUR CAPABILITIES OF CQ

CQ Drive is your interest and motivation to function in diverse cultural situations.

CQ Knowledge is your understanding of how cultures are similar and different.

CQ Strategy is your awareness and ability to plan for multicultural interactions.

CQ Action is your ability to appropriately adjust behaviour in different cultural contexts.

CHAPTER 2

Cultivating Connections: The Capabilities in Action

Disgusting?? Maybe it's just different!

CQ DRIVE

After a long-haul journey from North America to Asia, ending with a four-hour drive from the Mongolian capital city of Ulaanbaatar to the northern town of Dharkan, all I wanted to do was eat and sleep. But when we arrived in Dharkan my host had organized a meeting with a nomadic herder, and told me that we would be going to his place for lunch. I love meeting people from various cultures – it energizes me – but at this moment in time, I was extremely tired. I had been on the road for the last two weeks across Asia, and after being billeted with various generous hosts I was secretly craving my own space and familiar comforts.

As we pulled up to the ger (yurt), a friendly and extremely hospitable couple welcomed us into their home. There was a pot boiling in the middle of the ger which was filled with strange pieces of meat. The smell was overpowering, and as I was being seated, I found out through my translator that we were being served horse organs!

Once again, my goal was to develop meaningful relationships with this beautiful couple from Mongolia, so I kicked my CQ Drive into gear and persevered. While I didn't eat a huge amount, I listened attentively to my hosts as they explained the different organs I was nibbling at. I even worked up the courage to use the outdoor toilet, where the only thing that was keeping me from falling into the pit were a few planks! Working through this challenging cross-cultural situation led to smiles and laughter, which in turn led to deeper conversations and new friendships.

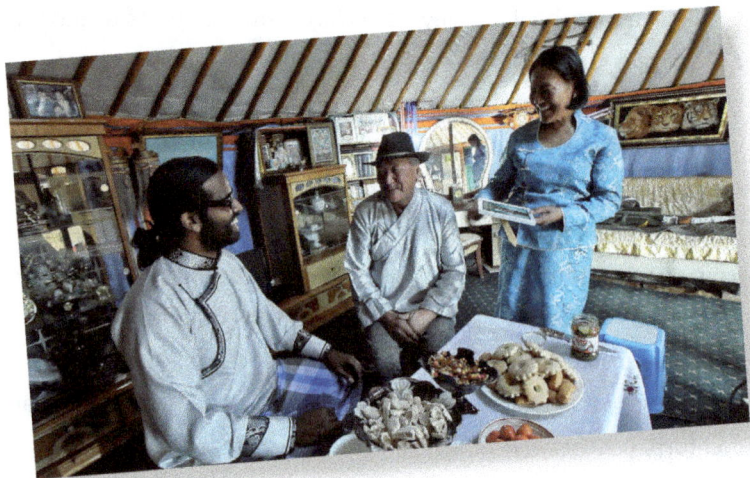

HOW TO INCREASE YOUR CQ DRIVE

- Look for things that interest you about another culture
- Step out of your comfort zone (face your biases)
- Interact with a culture that makes you feel uncomfortable
- Eat foods that you normally don't eat, and be honest in how you feel

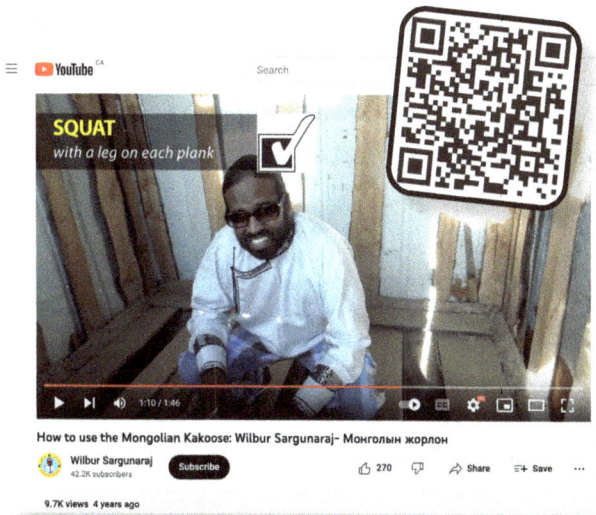

How to use the Mongolian Kakoose: Wilbur Sargunaraj- Монголын жорлон

Wilbur Sargunaraj
42.2K subscribers

Subscribe

270   Share   Save   ...

9.7K views 4 years ago

CQ KNOWLEDGE

I had come to the city of Iqaluit in Nunavut to perform and speak at a festival. The Territory of Nunavut is in Canada, and is home to the Inuit. While 'Eskimo' might be a common term to use for First Nations people in Alaska, the term Inuit is used in Canada. I thought I had done my homework and was ready to present at the event – it was July 1st, which meant Canada Day celebrations were underway across the country.

For some Indigenous people in Canada the celebration of Canada Day is a contentious issue because of the history of colonization and residential schools, so I decided to talk about reconciliation. This is a hard topic to talk about, but having worked with Indigenous colleagues in Canada on this topic I felt comfortable and excited to share my heart on what reconciliation means to me as a Settler.

After my talk and performance, which I thought had gone over very well, I was confronted by an Inuit woman who was not pleased with what I had to say. I tried to dialogue and understand what had offended her, but she walked away. Later I learned that some of the Inuit did not like the word reconciliation as they felt it was another patronizing agenda that was formulated and being pushed by the government.

I should have broadened my CQ Knowledge on how Inuit people feel about the term reconciliation, instead of relying on language familiar to me from conversations with First Nations people in Western Canada.

That evening I took a walk to reflect on the day, and by chance I met a group of Inuit who welcomed me into their humble home by the beach. As we sat together, they helped me to increase my CQ Knowledge, and I learned from my new friends that reconciliation was more about taking action than using buzz words. In those few hours under the midnight sun, my new Inuit friends taught me how we can come together and truly make reconciliation a reality.

HOW TO INCREASE YOUR CQ KNOWLEDGE

- Make friends with someone from another culture, and humbly ask questions
- Watch movies, read books, learn words, and listen to music from another culture
- Don't base your ideas about a culture on only one interaction
- Follow reputable global news sources
- Don't believe your culture is superior to others

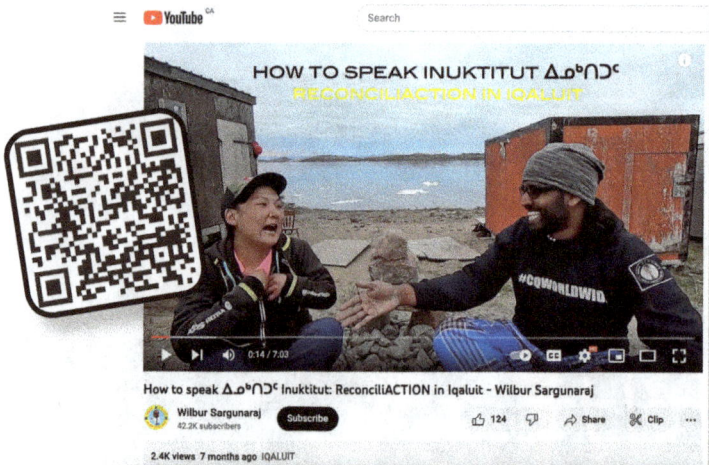

How to speak ᐃᓄᒃᑎᑐᑦ Inuktitut: ReconciliACTION in Iqaluit - Wilbur Sargunaraj

Wilbur Sargunaraj
42.2K subscribers

124 Share Clip

2.4K views 7 months ago IQALUIT

CQ STRATEGY

There was no time to adjust! There was no time to drop off bags at the hotel and no time to freshen up. I had just landed in Lusaka, Zambia and was heading directly to interview one of my friends, who was working as a Peace Ambassador for the United Nations High Commissioner for Refugees.

I arrived at a busy outdoor market, met my friend Isa, and started the interview. About five minutes into our conversation, a local shopkeeper interrupted us. He proceeded to drape the Zambian flag around me and said it looked great on me. Not wanting to disrespect him, or the flag, I started thinking to myself – is the shopkeeper trying to persuade me to buy this souvenir, or is he just trying to be nice and welcome me?

I'll be honest – I was frustrated, and thought he was just trying to make money from me, especially because of his interruption. Isa and I kept the camera rolling, and decided to have him join our conversation.

When the interview was over, I had a chat with the shopkeeper and realized all my negative assumptions were wrong. He just wanted to make me feel welcome, and thought a Zambian flag would be a great prop in the video! He went on to teach me some key phrases in the Nyanja language, and pointed me in the direction of his favourite places to eat. Thankfully I had slowed myself down, and by using CQ Strategy I managed to make a connection instead of judging someone and pushing them away.

HOW TO INCREASE YOUR CQ STRATEGY

When engaging with someone from another culture:

- Watch More
- Listen More
- Speak Less
- Don't judge but reflect: "I wonder why that is?"
- Ask questions

Issa Embombolo
Founder of Peace Clubs, Former Peace facilitator UNHCR, Lusaka, Zambia

How to make Peace: Wilbur Sargunaraj in Zambia

Wilbur Sargunaraj
43.7K subscribers

Analytics   Edit video

52   Share

CQ ACTION

While I was in Kenya, I was hoping to interview a few people from the Maasai tribe for a cultural intelligence video project. My hosts, who lived in Nairobi, said that certain Maasai were hesitant to meet foreigners because of tourists who were only interested in taking photos with them and then promptly moving on. When we arrived at the village my hosts managed to find someone who was willing to be part of the interview, but I could sense he was a bit reserved. I made sure the cameras were put away as I needed to establish a relationship first.

In Africa there are different ways to shake hands. Some handshakes involve snapping middle fingers, holding your own elbow or using both hands. I was aware that the Maasai had a different greeting, so I extended my hand and allowed him to take the lead. He smiled at me, gave a firm handshake and introduced himself as David.

I introduced myself and decided to use a little Tamil, as I felt this might pique his curiosity. He raised his eyebrows and asked me what language I spoke and where I came from. He spoke English very well, so I made sure that I didn't speak too slowly. I apologized for not coming prepared to speak a few words in his language, and I asked him to teach me basic phrases in Maa. As our conversation progressed, he realized that I was genuinely interested in getting to know him as a person.

Understanding that cows were an integral part of the Maasai culture, I told David that my dad came from a small agricultural village, and that I was surrounded by cows as a kid. His eyes lit up, and he started to talk with passion about how all the cows in Tamil Nadu – and the whole world, belonged to the Maasai!

We had a good laugh together, and by this time his friends who were watching seemed a bit jealous and wanted to be part of the conversation. David motioned for them to join us, and a wonderful cultural exchange ensued. We were having such a great time that I almost forgot to bring out the cameras. I asked for permission, to which I received an excited, resounding approval, and my new friends taught me the jumping Adumu dance – how to rest while balancing on one foot – and I in turn taught them the Dapakuthu dance and several Tamil words ... the good ones of course!

Once again by using CQ Action I was able to make a connection and have a meaningful and rich encounter with new friends.

HOW TO INCREASE YOUR CQ ACTION

- Be aware of cultural taboos
- Adjust your behaviour to cultural norms
- Speak at an appropriate pace
- Learn and use basic phrases
- Discover ways to build relationships through common ground

Wilbur in Kenya: How to say Greetings in Maasai

Wilbur Sargunaraj
42.2K subscribers

94

Share

17K views 12 years ago

MAKING MISTAKES IS OK

Making mistakes and feeling uncomfortable are all part of the journey as you learn and develop cross-cultural relationships. When you're connecting with someone from a different culture, go easy on yourself. You don't have to know everything or perform flawlessly in these cross-cultural settings. Eating different food, trying to speak a different language, and making conversations with someone from a different culture can all be overwhelming. Yet, you may be surprised how understanding people are when they see that you are making the effort to develop the relationship!

HOW'S YOUR CQ?

Having high cultural intelligence doesn't mean demonstrating perfect behaviour in cross-cultural interactions. As you can see from these stories, making mistakes and feeling overwhelmed are part of the journey in developing CQ.

People with a high CQ are not intimidated by differences, but try to learn from them. Every day we are presented with opportunities to rub shoulders with people from all around the world. With immigration and globalization on the rise, we don't have to board a plane to exercise cultural intelligence. Every day is a chance to step out of our comfort zones and develop relationships with people.

Sadly, humans have a natural inclination to feel fear toward things that are unfamiliar and different. We are quick to stereotype, judge, and push people away from us. This happens at our schools, at the grocery store, at work, at playgrounds, and in our day-to-day interactions with people. But by using CQ we can come together with all our differences, and work towards forming relationships.

While there are in depth self-assessments on the topic, here is a quick way to reflect on your CQ. Take a moment to consider the following statements. Don't worry about giving right or wrong answers, and be honest with yourself.

• I enjoy learning about different cultures.

• I like trying foods from different cultures.

• I appropriately adapt the way I speak when I meet people from other cultures.

• I have friends from many cultures.

• If people from a different culture than mine do things that I am not used to, I can avoid judging them.

- Before I meet someone from another culture, I usually plan how I will relate to them.

- I recently discovered a bias I had towards a certain culture.

- I enjoy talking to people who don't speak my language.

- I am confident that I can make friends with people whose cultural backgrounds are different than mine.

- I find cross-cultural experiences rewarding.

- When I hear ideas or something interesting about a different culture, I ask questions and observe to make sure they are factual.

- **Bonus Scenario!** I would be willing to try a South Asian squatting latrine without toilet paper. I would have no issue cleaning myself with water and my hands. I would also be comfortable using an African pit latrine and clean myself with leaves!

If you answered 'Yes' to the majority of these statements, it shows that you are a person who is exercising high cultural

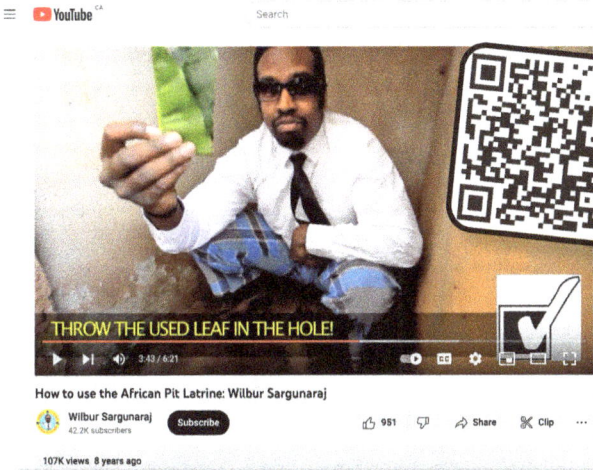

intelligence. If you answered 'No' to the majority of these scenarios, then you are where almost everyone starts! This is a great time to slowly work on increasing your CQ.

No matter where you are on the scale, you can work towards increasing your cultural intelligence using these four capabilities. Part of building your CQ Knowledge is understanding your own values in relation to others, and this is what we'll be exploring in the next chapter.

DISGUSTING OR DIFFERENT?

LOW CQ - You react: "Disgusting! How can those
people eat that!"

HIGH CQ – You recognize: "How interesting! This is
different for me!"

How to eat the Insects: Wilbur Sargunaraj in Phnom Penh, Cambodia

Wilbur Sargunaraj
42.2K subscribers

Subscribe

158

Share   Clip

5.1K views 5 years ago

WESTERN TOILET

INDIAN

CHAPTER 3
Cultural Values

Cultural intelligence always watches,
listens and is slow to speak.

WHAT ARE CULTURAL VALUES?

Cultural values are beliefs, attitudes, and preferences that are important to people within a culture or community. The cultural values and dimensions discussed in this chapter were described in the book *Cultures and Organizations* by social psychologist Geert Hofestede. Another model of cultural values was developed by Dutch organizational theorist Fons Trompenaars and by researchers in the GLOBE study. While we can use this system of values to analyze similarities and differences between cultures, it's important to understand the danger of stereotyping an entire culture. We cannot assume that every person within a particular culture will behave or think the same way, as there will be people within a larger culture that are exceptions to the norm. Not all Indians have a high power distance orientation, (placing a strong emphasis on hierarchy and status) and not all Americans will be individualistic. Keep in mind that one cultural value is not necessarily superior or inferior than another. Having personal preferences for certain values is normal. It is important to have an open mind, a willingness to learn, and respect for other cultural values.

In this chapter I will share a story or personal experience that will help explain each of the values. Reflect on these cultural dimensions and how they are a part of your own values. How can your understanding of these values help you to develop relationships with people who may have different cultural values than your own?

CULTURAL VALUES

Doing — Being

Context

Affective — Neutral

Individualism — Collectivism

Monochronic — Polychronic

Competitive — Cooperative

Power Distance

Uncertainty Avoidance

Time Orientation

Universalism — Particularism

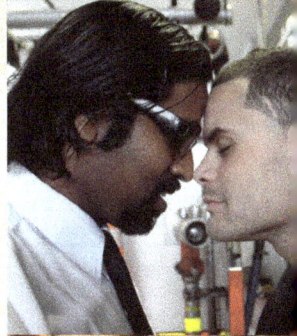

DOING - BEING

Does one work to live or live to work? This value can be defined as the extent to which **results** and **actions** are emphasized and valued. People in doing-oriented countries like Canada, the United Kingdom, or Germany, place importance on being busy and task-focused, prioritizing efficiency and results. In comparison, people in being-oriented countries like Brazil, Sweden, or the Arab cluster, place importance on the enjoyment and quality of life. Family takes precedence over work.

I remember the time I was in Cagliari, Italy, to create a series of cultural intelligence videos. Our days involved running around the town to different locations and meeting people. Despite the fact that we had an extremely busy schedule, I followed my host as we stopped at a café almost every half hour to visit and socialize with friends. There were times he would recognize a familiar face, and — even if it was just for five minutes — there would be a coffee break to connect with people. I noticed it wasn't so much the coffee that made people stop (don't get me wrong, the coffee was first class!) but the fact that people in a being-oriented culture like Italy place a huge emphasis on the quality of life. It's almost as if the socializing at the café, and the work we were doing, went hand-in-hand.

Fast-forward to a few years later, when I was in doing-oriented Germany. A company had hired me to conduct workshops and participate in a few meetings at their headquarters. We carefully followed a very meticulously organized schedule (which was sent almost 2 months in advance!) – there was no time to be wasted, and certainly there was no time for multiple improvised coffee breaks! After the morning meeting we broke for lunch, and because I tend to be more of a being-oriented person, I ate my schnitzel slowly, thinking that I could use this time to get to know my hosts. I thought we were just at the beginning of a conversation, when one of my hosts looked at her watch and said that we had to move on to the next meeting. I still had half a sausage left on my plate, and my hosts had already completed their meal, so I quickly gobbled what was left and wondered what happened to nice conversations over coffee!

I looked at the schedule and yes, there was time for coffee, but it was only for ten minutes in the mid-afternoon. In the end I did have my coffee, but there was no socializing or loud laughs over Lavazza! It was definitely not like the coffee breaks I experienced in Italy! At the end of the day, one of the kind German associates said, "Mr. Wilbur, thank you for coming – it was an extremely productive and efficient day!" It sure was!

Doing – Being

Cappuccino: More coffee less milk

2:29 / 5:13

Wilbur in Cagliari: Typical Italian Coffee Break

CONTEXT

People in low-context countries like Switzerland, the United States, and the Netherlands value direct communication and explicit words, while people from high-context countries like Japan, China, and Saudi Arabia are known for using indirect communication and reading between the lines. In many high-context cultures, 'saving face' is an important practice to ensure that your dignity and the dignity of others is kept. Etiquette, manners, and how you behave publicly all become very important.

There were only 45 minutes left before the plane was supposed to land. The cabin crew had just finished serving breakfast, and our in-flight movies were interrupted by a special message from the Australia Border Force. This was my first time 'Down Under' so I was curious what kind of welcome I would receive.

Ominous music started, and large text flashed on the screen accompanied with a low voice that said 'Declare or Beware'. A man dressed in military uniform with an Australian accent proceeded to speak with a stern voice, which reached right into my heart and soul. I heard the phrase 'Declare or Beware' almost three or four times before the video ended and the screen went back to our movies.

I had no desire to finish the movie now! I was too busy thinking

– did I have any food items in my suitcase? Did my mom secretly pack garlic pickle? Did she smuggle some delicious chicken curry in my checked baggage? I was convinced I hadn't brought anything that would be an issue, but I was still rattled by this stern welcome from the Australian Border Force. There would be no misunderstanding. The message was clear explicit and direct – Wilbur, you must Declare or Beware!

Countries like Australia or America are extremely direct in their communication, and people from high-context countries often find this unsettling. It is equally unsettling for people from low-context cultures to navigate high-context communication, where one must read between the lines to catch the nuances of communication. Japan is one of the most high-context countries in the world, where one has to infer what is being communicated.

When I lived in Japan, I wanted to make sure I didn't become a 'kuki yomenai' – 空気読めない – a phrase which translates to 'one who cannot read the air'. This was easier said than done! It was extremely complicated to navigate communication in Japan – from offering something to a Japanese person to asking them an honest opinion, I had to learn how to interpret their responses.

I remember a time when one of my Japanese friends stopped talking to me for a while. I sent an email to him asking why, and based on his reply, it was clear that I had done something to offend him – but no details were given. As a person from a high-context culture it was difficult for him to be direct with me, and I was probably making him feel even more uncomfortable by asking for clear communication. In the end I was left to pour over our email messages to find clues to discern what mistake I had made. I confess I couldn't read between the lines!

I heard about another story from Kyoto, where a businessman had a meeting with a client who complimented the businessman on his watch. The businessman started to talk about the watch; but then realized that the compliment had been a cue to look down at his watch, see the time, and end the meeting!

Something similar could happen in India, another high-context culture, where people also have to read the air. Indians regularly communicate using body language, and the Indian head wobble/shake is a great example. That one movement can mean yes, maybe, no, or just "I'm listening", and one has to read between the lines to understand what is being implied.

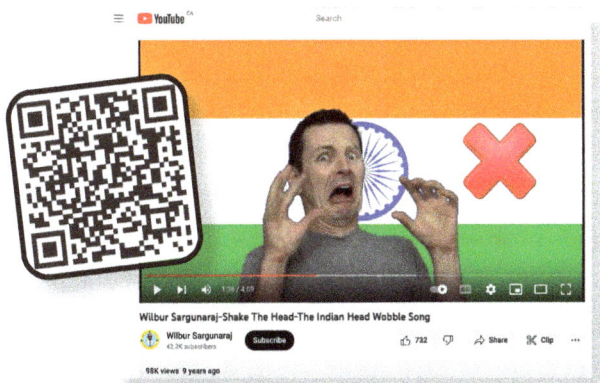

Wilbur Sargunaraj-Shake The Head-The Indian Head Wobble Song
Wilbur Sargunaraj
98K views 9 years ago

AFFECTIVE - NEUTRAL

This value is all about how you express yourself. Affective cultures like the French or Italians express their feelings very openly. In these countries people tend to be animated and enthusiastic, and use physical gestures for communication. People from neutral-oriented cultures like Ethiopia, Japan, or the United Kingdom don't easily express their emotions or reveal how they feel. Emotional outbursts are usually frowned upon.

Have you ever been to an Indian funeral? You may have had the chance to attend an Indian wedding in all its glory, but there is something to be said for witnessing an Indian funeral as well. The house where I grew up in Madurai was literally a few yards away from an open-air cremation ground. Almost every day there would be a body that was carried in a grand procession with garlands, flowers, drummers, and fireworks, all accompanied by people wailing.

I remember being at a relative's funeral where one of my aunts was wailing intensely. When she noticed I wasn't crying, she stopped abruptly, looked at me with a confused look, resumed hitting her head with the palm of both hands, and said in Tamil "Wilbur, Cry! Wail! You need to wail out loud!" People in India are expressive! We are an affective group of people and we let people know how we feel at weddings, funerals, and all the moments in between!

One thing that I found fascinating upon moving to North America was how people would do everything to restrain themselves at funerals. It's a solemn and quiet event. I would hear the occasional whimper but it was pretty much 'neutral' in terms of emotional expression. Once again, we can't stereotype and say all Indians are affective, as I am sure there are people who are quiet, calm, and express their feelings in a more subdued way ... but many of us like to wail!

INDIVIDUALISM - COLLECTIVISM

Individual goals and rights are extremely important in countries like Canada, the United States, and Australia. In comparison, collectivist countries like Uganda, India, and China focus on personal relationships and the importance of the group. This can be seen in the Māori concept of 'whanaungatanga' (relationships/ connections) and the African philosophy 'ubuntu', which means 'I am because of we.' If there is one cultural value that really defines the Anglo cluster, it would be individualism. This value also helps us to understand why personal space is so important in these cultures.

The Covid-19 pandemic really brought out stark differences between individualistic and collectivist countries, and this was highly evident when it came to masking and the use of vaccination mandates by governments. When I lived in Japan in 2005, I remember instances on the Tokyo Metro where many people were masked. Mask wearing is a long-established practice and is a common courtesy, even if someone has something as harmless as a common cold. In collectivist countries the actions of individuals matter not just for themselves, but to protect the larger community and their country – so mask-wearing was an easy order to follow during the pandemic. On the other hand, when mask mandates were announced in individualistic countries, there was uproar and anger as personal rights are of the utmost importance. Being told to wear a mask was seen as taking someone's freedom away, or quite literally muzzling them. I recall when these mandates were lifted, a friend of mine celebrated by making a video on social media in which he used a blow-torch to incinerate his mask collection!

Another good example of individualism and collectivism is seen in families. Collectivist cultures, particularly in Asia, place an emphasis on the importance of familial relationships, which means it's not uncommon to see large extended family units living together in one house. When I moved to Canada, I remember being surprised that several of my peers in high school were anxious to get their drivers licenses and move out of their parents' homes. From a young age people in individualistic countries are taught to value their independence.

Candy Yam
Sweet Potato cooked with butter and sugar

How to eat the "Soul Food"- Wilbur Sargunaraj in Chicago

Wilbur Sargunaraj
43.7K subscribers

273   Share

MONOCHRONIC - POLYCHRONIC

In monochronic countries like Canada, Germany, or Australia, people believe that events should happen in order – one task at a time. Being punctual, having agendas, and keeping to schedules are all extremely important. Contrast this with countries in Sub-Saharan Africa where people can work on multiple tasks at the same time, and where work and personal life are woven together. Relationships, the community, and time spent with family are extremely important.

I had an engagement to perform and speak at a community event on the outskirts of Lusaka, Zambia, scheduled to commence at 10 am. My host made sure we arrived early, and I was seated right up at the front at 9:30am. I started chatting with some people for a while, and at around ten o'clock I started looking for cues to take the stage. It was a packed hall, but things didn't seem like they were going to start anytime soon! I asked my host if we were delayed, and he said, "of course not"! We were just waiting for a few more people.

Time dragged on. By 10:30 I was really fidgety, and when eleven o'clock came and went, I was ready to leave! I asked my host again when we might be starting, and he said "soon". Well, "soon" turned out to be two and a half hours later! During this time (while totally agitated) I observed how people were chatting with one another and enjoying their time together. People from monochronic countries would find this extremely frustrating, as they are used to schedules, and doing one thing at a time. Meanwhile, people from polychronic countries adapt well to interruptions and changes, placing value on the interpersonal relationships.

This is maybe what could explain the stereotypical notion of 'African Time'. This is quite common in many other cultures too, where we can see 'Hawaiian Time', 'Colombian Time' and of course IST in India. Indian Standard Time is an actual time zone, but for many of us in India it also has another meaning – how late you show up to an event! It is guaranteed that my family would win the 'showing up late' prize. In fact, there should be a dedicated time zone poking fun at our family! I remember that we would show up consistently an hour late to family gatherings when I was a kid, and trying to arrive on time at the railway station was futile! The only event we started precisely on time was church – maybe this is because our church services (just like in the African continent) are always 3 to 4 hours long and need all the time they can get! Though I grew up in a polychronic culture, I still have not mastered the art of enduring long meandering public events!

Dunk-a-Chicken (The Village Way) - Wilbur Sargunaraj

Wilbur Sargunaraj
42.2K subscribers

Subscribe

849

Share

Clip

Monochronic -
Polychronic

COMPETITIVE - COOPERATIVE

People from countries like Singapore, Germany, and the United States are very competitive – which means they place an emphasis on achievements, competition, and getting tasks done. In comparison, people from cooperative countries in the Nordic Europe cluster or in Sub-Saharan Africa, place an emphasis on relationships, family, and working together. Cooperative cultures focus on 'being' as opposed to 'doing'. Time is a bit more loose, and life is often more relaxed.

I took one look at the results and my heart dropped. No, it wasn't a doctor's report – it was my grade 8 class ranking results. After all the exams we had written at my school in India, it was time to see who was the best. There were 63 of us in the class and I came in at 13. One would think that would be a cause for celebration – but all my effort didn't matter. I was reduced to a number, and there were twelve others who had been better than me.

Indian parents want their child to be number one, and the pressure put on children is immense. In grade 10 your marks and rank determine what you go on to study in higher education. Because of this pressure to pass exams, it's common to hear about young students taking their lives after seeing their results. Students are assigned a number, and your results are posted in the newspaper. If your number does not appear, you have failed – and your whole world comes crashing down. The drive to achieve is common across South Asia. Competitive societies believe ranking and grades may help kids excel, but many young students complain of burnout and the extreme pressure to achieve. This is observed in Singapore, which is one of the most competitive countries in the world.

Meanwhile, cooperative countries in Scandinavia are quite modest, where 'Jante' or 'Janteloven' plays out. This is a code of conduct that encourages people to believe that they are not better than anyone else. One of my friends from Denmark mentioned that there are no elite programs for 'gifted' students, and that working as a group is considered more important than standing out as an individual. This is in stark contrast to India or America, where climbing the ladder of personal greatness and success is commonplace. After struggling with the competitive Indian school system, I now realize that cooperative values are more meaningful to me, and I appreciate the philosophy of ubuntu, where life is lived in community and we all cross the finish line together!

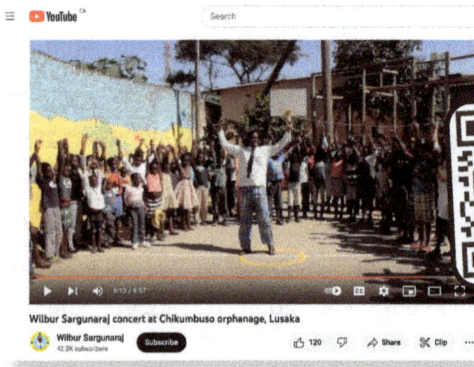

Wilbur Sargunaraj concert at Chikumbuso orphanage, Lusaka
Wilbur Sargunaraj

POWER DISTANCE

Power distance is the extent to which power and status
are expected and accepted. People in low power distance
countries like New Zealand, Norway, and Israel shy away
from titles and roles, and focus on equality across all levels.
In comparison, people in high power distance countries
like Malaysia and the Philippines place a strong emphasis
on hierarchy and status, and people with power are rarely
challenged. High power distance can also be seen within
the caste system in India, where there is extreme inequality
between the powerful and less powerful.

If you walk the streets of a middle-class neighbourhood in Tamil
Nadu, you will see something quite interesting. At most homes,
the owners' names are carved into the compound wall or beside
their front door. The interesting thing is that people don't stop
with names, but also list educational credentials, places of work,
and their job title! These overt references to status are also
seen when people list educational credentials on their wedding
invitation – the more degrees the better!

Power distance can also be seen in how people address one
another. Growing up in India I was taught to never call my uncles
or aunts by their first name but use honorific Tamil titles. If I ever
used their first names, I knew I would be in big trouble, and when
I moved to low power distance Canada, I found it extremely

difficult to call someone by their first name. I called everyone Sir / Madam or uncle / auntie (even if they were not related to me). One of my guardians found it quite uncomfortable when I insisted that I could only call her 'Aunty' instead of addressing her by her first name Betty! In the end we settled for 'Aunty Betty'!

Emphasis on hierarchy and status is evident in various countries, especially in Asia. In the 1980's, after a string of Korean Air aviation disasters, investigators finally attributed these accidents to high power distance issues. In many cases the root issue was that junior pilots did not want to speak up or contradict their senior officers, even though they knew how to avert the disaster. Following this, Korean Air implemented specific CRM (Crew Resource Management) training to prevent such issues, and has enjoyed an excellent safety record ever since. Cultures with high power distance grant power to those on top of the ladder, while people at the bottom must follow the social order of respecting those in power and deferring to them.

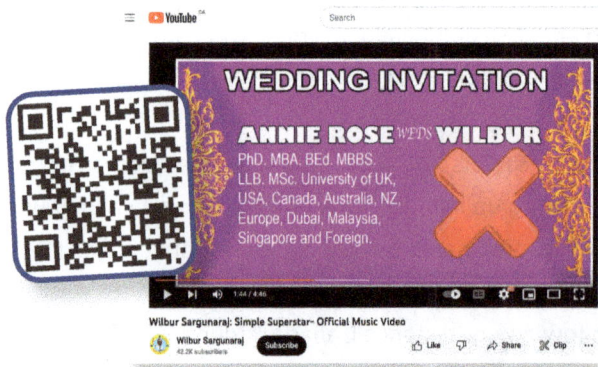

Wilbur Sargunaraj: Simple Superstar~ Official Music Video

UNCERTAINTY AVOIDANCE

Uncertainty-avoidance is the degree to which people in a society feel comfortable or uncomfortable in ambiguous situations. It is the extent to which risk is reduced or avoided. People in low uncertainty-avoidance countries like India, Jamaica, and Sweden are generally very adaptable. These cultures are usually comfortable with change and unpredictable situations. They are also usually comfortable with risk-taking, and operating with few rules. People in high uncertainty-avoidance countries like Poland, Italy, and Russia tend to avoid change, take calculated risks, and give importance to structure. High uncertainty-avoidance cultures are likely to have measures that mitigate unknown situations.

Bob Marley's *Three Little Birds*, is a fitting song for Jamaica, which is one of the lowest uncertainty-avoidance countries. In the face of uncertainty ... 'everything is going to be alright'! Of course, it helps that Jamaica has beautiful beaches, rolling mountains, reggae, and that genuine laid-back vibe. Thailand has a similar phrase, 'mai pen rai' which translates to Jamaica's 'everything is ok' or 'no worries'. In Tamil Nadu we also use the Tanglish (Tamil and English mixed) phrase, 'adjust panungae', which would translate to 'just adjust'. We use this term with others who are in unpredictable situations, or when we need people to be flexible.

Low uncertainty-avoidance countries usually have lower stress levels, and know how to handle 'romba tension' (another Tanglish word for being stressed)! There is a much more relaxed attitude to rules, and there is a general acceptance of the new and unusual. People in countries with high uncertainty-avoidance may enjoy security and stability, but they frequently have higher stress and anxiety levels because they feel threatened by unknown or ambiguous situations.

While there are multiple factors involved, there is a correlation between a country's acceptance of outsiders and its uncertainty-avoidance. Japan is one of the highest uncertainty-avoidance countries, which means that sometimes diversity can be seen as a potential source of conflict. An outsider can be perceived as someone who brings values and beliefs that may clash with a high uncertainty-avoidance country's stability and norms, creating a sense of anxiety.

While Japan has taken steps to work on this issue, I remember seeing this play out with the infamous 'gaijin card' – which has now been renamed. The term 'gaijin' means 'alien' or 'outside person', and every foreigner coming into the country had to be in possession of the card. While it is not an inherently derogatory term, the word 'gaijin' can be used in ways which suggest that foreigners are possibly inferior to Japanese people, and I remember being stopped a number of times by the authorities (of course in the most polite Japanese way) to show them my alien card. I was stopped in the Tokyo Metro, on the busy streets of Roppongi, and even in the quiet streets of Chiba when I was walking back to my apartment.

I got so used to interacting with the police that I could predict which ones would stop me. I remember a time at Narita airport in Tokyo, when two police officers were walking back and forth and taking suspicious glances at me. Before they could even make their move, I went up to them and with the biggest smile flashed my card and said politely, "Konnichiwa! Kore ga watashi no Gaijin Card des! Domo!" (Hello! Here is my Gaijin card. Thank you!) The officers bowed and repeatedly said "Sumimasen! Sumimasen!" (Excuse me/sorry).

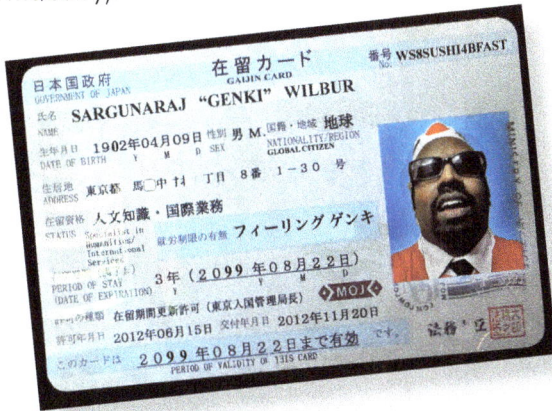

Countries with low uncertainty-avoidance like India are usually open to change and diversity. Being comfortable with the unknown can help people in these countries to interact with people who are different than themselves. That being said, there are still ongoing conflicts between castes and religions, where tensions between Hindus and Muslims still exist. Low uncertainty-avoidance can sometimes be seen in traffic, especially in India, where neither driving or being a pedestrian is for the faint of heart! While it may seem chaotic, there is an unseen choreography taking place between honking vehicles, street vendors and animals. There are 'rules', but they are viewed more as suggestions than absolutes, and risk-taking is normal. People cross multiple lanes of traffic, at any place and at any time, and weave in and out of the oncoming vehicles as needed. A tip for crossing India's daunting and busy streets is to sing Bob Marley's, "everything's gonna be alright" while you close your eyes and step into the great unknown!

Wilbur Sargunaraj - Feeling Genki (フィーリング ゲンキ)

TIME ORIENTATION

Time orientation is how a society or culture values time. People in countries like Japan, China, or South Korea focus on long-term planning, and are willing to sacrifice short-term benefits for prosperity in the future. People in short-term time orientation countries like the United Kingdom, Iceland, or Australia focus on the present, and are interested in achieving results immediately or in the near future. In short-term time orientation cultures, "Time is money!" In long-term time orientation cultures, the old adage applies – "Rome wasn't built in a day"!

Japan is one of the most long-term time-oriented countries in the world, and it values long-term interactions and associations. You can see this in the Japanese business world, where many companies are not focused on making an immediate profit, but are focused on the longevity of the company and how it can serve people in future generations. Japanese companies like Nintendo, Mitsubishi, Toshiba, and others have been around for over a hundred years.

I remember having meetings in Funabashi with a potential client who took me out to lunch and dinner on multiple occasions, where we would have lengthy conversations about personal interests and hobbies. He even invited me a number of times to his home to meet his family. It was only after my client felt that we had established mutual trust and a good relationship that I was hired for the project, and our friendship is quite strong to this day. Similarly, 'nomikai', or the practice of socializing after work, is prevalent in Japan. It helps maintain loyalty and trust within a company, with the hope of creating a long-term commitment.

Another good example of long-term time orientation would be the seventh-generation principle held by the Haudenosaunee First Nation in North America. According to this philosophy, the decisions that are made today should have a positive impact for seven future generations. This not only applies to the stewardship of natural resources like water or land, but to human relationships as well.

In the Arab cluster, there is a focus on the short-term and the present. The common phrase "Inshallah" (God willing), denotes a belief that the future is already determined, which means there is less of an emphasis on long-term planning. I remember visiting Oman and planning a series of events across the Middle East. My Omani host was excited to plan a concert tour, so we started talking about logistics. Almost every question I had regarding proposed dates was answered with "Inshallah", and after a while I began to wonder how we would get this project off the ground. I admit I was starting to get frustrated with this response. But I remembered that, when I was growing up, my parents also immersed me in the idea that the future is uncertain so we need to leave it in God's hands. I also remembered that human interaction often takes priority over business objectives in the Arab world. Recalling this allowed me to exercise a little more patience as I strived to work with my Omani host. In the end, the project never did materialize, but the experience helped me to better understand the tensions and challenges when working with people who have a different time-orientation!

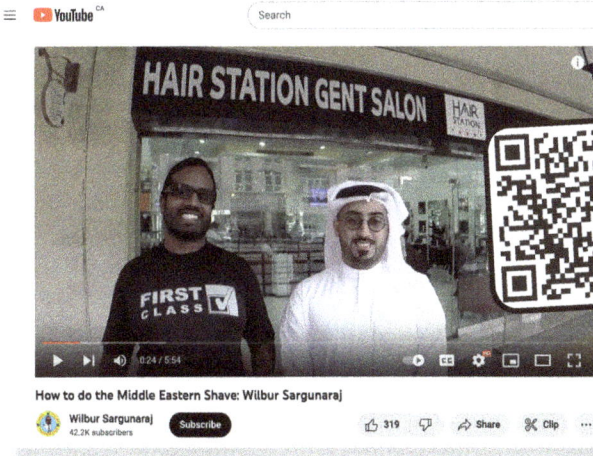

How to do the Middle Eastern Shave: Wilbur Sargunaraj
Wilbur Sargunaraj
42.2K subscribers

UNIVERSALISM - PARTICULARISM

What is more important to a culture – rules or relationships?
Universalism means that everybody is subject to the same
rules, and treated equally. People believe that laws and rules
should apply to everyone, including the wealthy and powerful,
and when exceptions are made, people feel frustrated. This
value is culturally normal in the Nordic Europe cluster and
in countries like Canada, Germany, and the United States.
Particularism means that circumstances dictate how rules
should be applied, and people are not treated equally. In a
strongly particularistic society like India, rules differ depending
on the person and their relationships with others, and you can
bypass rules if you know the right people.

I was standing at a long line at the check-in counter at Kolkata
Airport, where only one agent had the difficult task of checking
in a sea of passengers. She seemed stressed, and was doing
her best to get people to their flight on time, but I could sense
frustration among the passengers in the queue. As time slowly
moved on, I saw a disgruntled businessman walk from the back
of the line to interrupt the agent, who was dealing with another
passenger. "I am going to be late! Why are you taking so long!"
he openly and unashamedly yelled. The agent said, "I am sorry
sir, I am helping a customer". The businessman became more

aggressive with the agent, and began to say things like, "I want to speak to your manager," and "Do you know who I am?" I have heard this phrase spoken countless times in India, and it always frustrates me when people use power or status to receive preferential treatment. India is a high power distance and particularist country, where VIP culture is the norm. Politicians enjoy parading in their fancy cars, surrounded by blaring sirens and massive entourages to make their presence known! Indians find it fascinating when people who are powerful subject themselves to the same rules and behaviour as the common person. This is the reason why a royal from a Scandinavian country carrying their own suitcase while traveling, or a politician in Europe biking to work, makes news in India!

In India it's all about who you know. Using relationships to bend rules and get things done is a part of daily life. My parents always had someone to call to deal with banking, medical and legal needs. I had a distant uncle in Madurai who worked as a police officer, and to this day I am not sure what his rank was, but whenever my parents ran into difficulty, they would use his name. They used his status to get through checkpoints, to get better parking spots, to get special passes on trains and even to get to the front of the line. If a relative would get into a sticky situation, "better call Rajan Mama"! I have a friend in Canada who is a police officer, and I can't imagine asking him to give me special privileges or get me out of a speeding ticket! It just wouldn't be appropriate in universalistic North America!

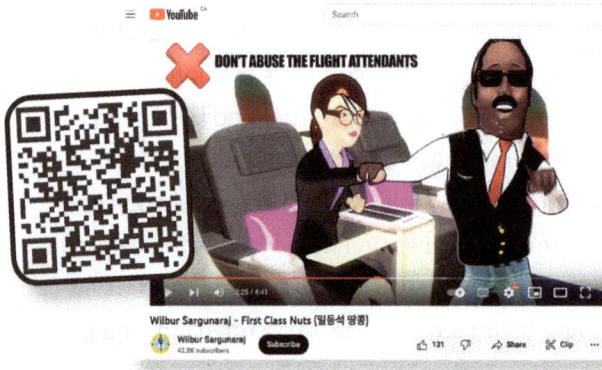

As we wrap up this chapter, I would like to say again that having a basic understanding of these values is a starting point to understanding different cultures, but it is important not to reduce these complex cultures to simplistic descriptions. While they can be helpful in understanding behaviours which you might witness within a culture, it's important to test any cultural stereotypes we have formed and always be ready to adjust our perceptions about other cultures as we start to interact with individual people in specific contexts.

While I always thought Australia was a highly individualistic country, it was only when I was on the ground interacting with people in specific contexts that I discovered that not all Australians line up with the cultural values that are attributed to them. We can use our knowledge of cultural values to better understand a society generally, but we need to take a thoughtful approach as we use them, being open to differences as we connect with individuals. The next chapter will take us around the world to understand different cultural clusters. These clusters – areas where certain cultural values are held by a number of different peoples and countries – can help us to grow a better understanding of large cultural groupings found across our world. Having a general understanding of these cultural values and clusters can help you increase your CQ Knowledge – but always remember that cultural knowledge needs to be coupled with your CQ Drive, a CQ Strategy and personal action in order to effectively build cross-cultural relationships!

WHERE ARE YOU FROM?

The question, "Where are you from?" can seem innocent, but it can be complicated – it often questions a person's sense of belonging in a particular place or setting, implying that they are different, or 'other'. The question may be posed because a person has a different accent, or skin colour, so the assumption is they must not be from 'here'. Asking questions like "tell me more about yourself", "how long have you lived in this city?", or "did you grow up here?" may be better ways of finding out more about someone you meet.

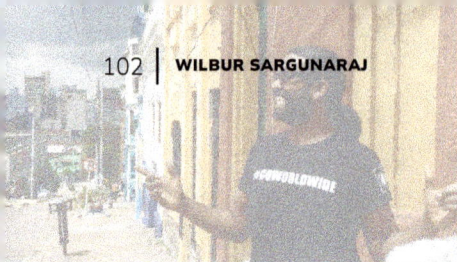

CHAPTER 4
The Cultural Clusters

*"The wide world is all about you: you
can fence yourselves in, but you cannot
forever fence it out."*

J.R.R Tolkien

WHAT IS A CULTURAL CLUSTER?

Clusters are cultural groupings where people often share
similar language, history, geography and religion. The
nations and groupings in these clusters also have shared beliefs
and similar cultural values. No grouping is complete or definitive,
as there are countries and cultures that don't fit neatly into these
clusters. For example, the European Baltic states, Caribbean, and
Pacific Island nations do not easily fit into these broad clusters.
Other researchers who have written about the cultural clusters

have not included a separate category for Indigenous peoples. In discussions with several Indigenous individuals, they often wondered why they were not included. Based on this feedback, I have offered a description of an Indigenous cluster, as many of these peoples share similar values and the same struggles resulting from colonization.

It's so important to say again that, while we might like to place cultures in neat categorizations, we cannot assume that every person within a particular culture will behave or think the same way. The nations I have listed in each of the clusters are where there is a high concentration of these cultural groupings. These clusters cannot, and aren't meant to, convey the immense diversity found across various countries and cultures; but can be a great place to begin comparing predominant worldviews in different contexts. Exploring the clusters is a useful starting point to understand differences and similarities between cultures which can help you effectively engage in cross-cultural situations.

CULTURAL CLUSTERS

CONFUCIAN ASIA
China, Japan, South Korea, etc.

SOUTHERN ASIA
India, Pakistan, Philippines, Sri Lanka,
Thailand, etc.

ARAB
Saudi Arabia, Egypt, Oman,
United Arab Emirates, etc.

SUB-SARAHAN AFRICA
Rwanda, Kenya, Zambia, Zimbabwe,
Nigeria, etc.

NORDIC EUROPE
Greenland, Denmark, Sweden, Finland, etc.

EASTERN EUROPE
Greece, Russia, Poland, Hungary, etc.

GERMANIC EUROPE
Germany, Netherlands, German speaking-
Switzerland, Austria, etc.

LATIN EUROPE
Italy, France, Spain, Portugal, etc.

ANGLO
United States, Canada, Australia, United Kingdom,
New Zealand, etc.

LATIN AMERICA
Brazil, Colombia, Mexico, Venezuela, etc.

INDIGENOUS
Māori, Inuit, Hawaiian, Aboriginal and Torres Strait Islander peoples etc.

CONFUCIAN ASIA

China, Japan, South Korea and other countries.

The philosophy of Confucius brings many of the countries in this cluster together. The teachings, rituals and practices described by the word 'Li' are engrained in society which includes great reverence for elders and deep respect for superiors. 关系, or guanxi (gwan-shee), is also at the heart of how society functions and gets things done. The word can be translated to mean 'connections', or 'who you know', and it plays an important role in these societies which tend to be highly collectivist. The Confucian Asia cluster is also known for being very high-context in communication style, where reading between the lines and saving face are very important.

Things to consider:

The importance of long-term trust building, good manners, showing respect, and polite introductions and greetings.

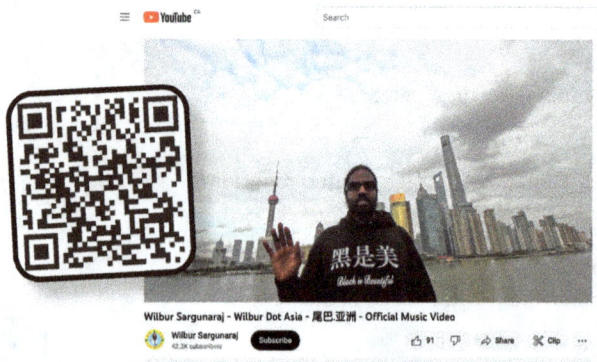

Wilbur Sargunaraj - Wilbur Dot Asia - 尾巴.亚洲 - Official Music Video
Wilbur Sargunaraj

With students from Baoding, Hebei at the Great Wall, Mutianyu, China

SOUTHERN ASIA

India, Pakistan, Philippines, Sri Lanka, Thailand and other countries.

The Southern Asian cluster is extremely diverse, with multiple cultures and religions. Even within the country of India, there are major differences between states in language, attire, and cuisine. While there are numerous differences in this cluster, cultures within it share some cultural values, including high power distance, consistently placing an importance on status and hierarchy. These cultures are collectivist, with high value placed on family and personal relationships.

Things to consider:

People keep small interpersonal space, value hierarchy, and hold religion to be very important.

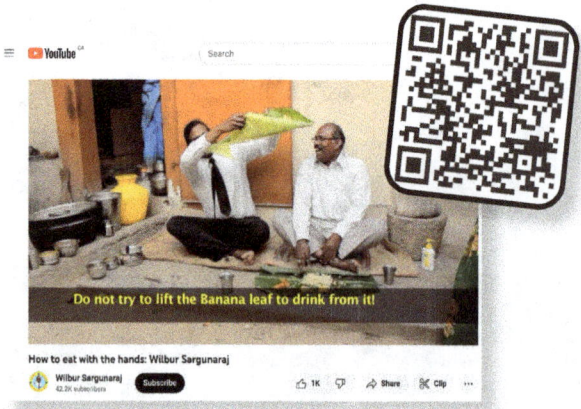

Do not try to lift the Banana leaf to drink from it!

How to eat with the hands: Wilbur Sargunaraj

With residents of the Ponnagam Old Age Home, Virudhunagar, Tamil Nadu, India

ARAB

Saudi Arabia, Egypt, Oman, United Arab Emirates, and other countries.

Islam plays an important role in the Arab cluster in the Middle East. Some countries in North Africa, including Egypt, Morocco, and Tunisia also fall into this grouping. People from these conservative countries are often collectivist, placing emphasis on family and the tribe. The Arab cluster demonstrates high power distance, which can be seen in the patriarchal structure of the family.

Things to consider:

The importance of Islam, daily prayer, not consuming pork or alcohol, and maintaining a conservative society.

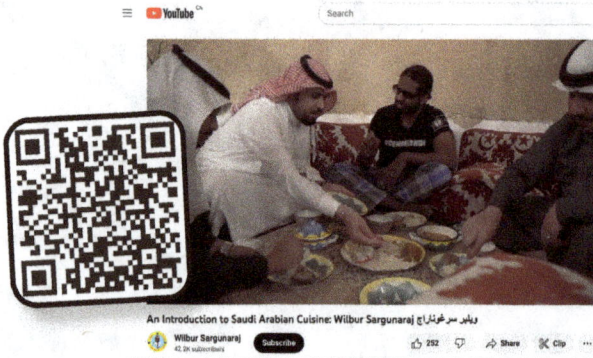

An Introduction to Saudi Arabian Cuisine: Wilbur Sargunaraj ويلبر سرغوناراج

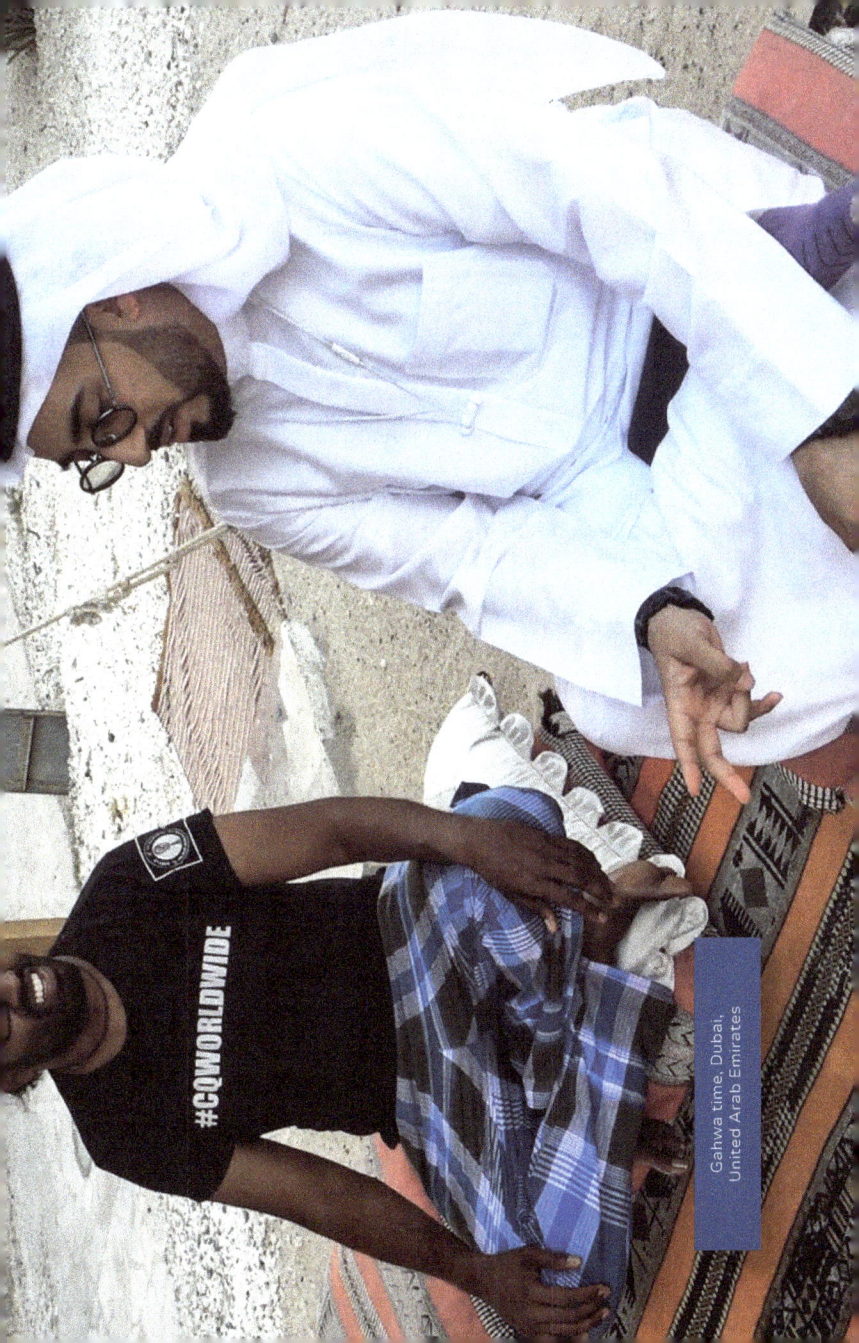

Gahwa time, Dubai,
United Arab Emirates

SUB-SAHARAN AFRICA

Rwanda, Kenya, Zambia, Zimbabwe, Nigeria and other countries.

This cluster is comprised of countries that lie south of the Sahara in Africa. 'Sub-Saharan' is a term used to distinguish countries that are not part of North Africa, as many of the North African countries fall into the Arab cluster due to the importance of Islam. Several cultures in the Sub-Saharan cluster are polychronic, and have a fluid orientation towards time, making this a 'being' rather than a 'doing' cluster. Personal and work lives here are often woven together. Countries in the Sub-Saharan cluster score high on the collectivist scale, as there is an emphasis placed on family and the group. The philosophy of ubuntu is woven through this cluster – here, the WE is more important than the I.

Things to consider:

The importance of 'ubuntu' (community), modesty, polychronic time, and family.

How to dance Kiganda: Wilbur in Uganda
Wilbur Sargunaraj

Kiganda lesson from students in Matugga, Uganda

NORDIC EUROPE

Greenland, Denmark, Sweden, Finland, and other countries.

One of the unifying characteristics of the Nordic Europe cluster is a love of minimalism. Scandinavian design and architecture focus on clean lines, simplicity, and functionality. While these countries are lumped together, there are some notable differences between them. People in Sweden often value independence, while people in Denmark and Norway tend to be more collectivist. *Janteloven* is a code of conduct that guides how people in this cluster behave with one another and how they view themselves. This philosophy means that behaviour in the Nordic cluster is generally modest, egalitarian, and characterised by care for the interests of the group instead of the individual. The cluster is also very universalistic, with everyone being subject to the same rules.

Things to consider:

The importance of punctuality, minimalism, and collectivist approaches to behaviour.

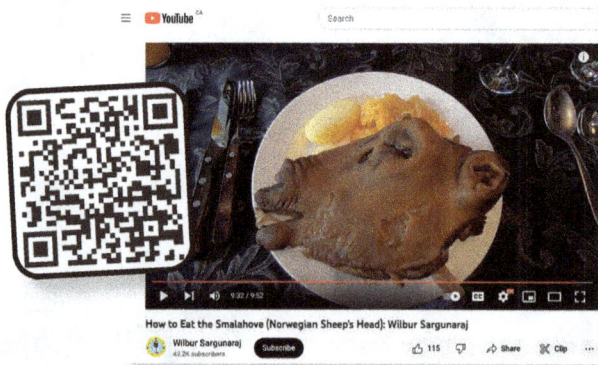

How to Eat the Smalahove (Norwegian Sheep's Head): Wilbur Sargunaraj

EASTERN EUROPE

Greece, Russia, Poland, Hungary and other countries.

The Eastern European cluster is another grouping that is extremely diverse. Part of this cluster lies in Europe (e.g. Poland, European Russia) and the other part in Asia (e.g. Georgia, Asian Russia). The cultural backgrounds of different countries here are varied which include Slavic, Turk-Muslim, and Greek. Countries within this cluster share a history of colonization, both from cultures outside the cluster and from cultures within it. They also share the influence of the Byzantine Empire which is reflected in the establishment of Eastern Orthodox churches in many of the countries. The Eastern European cluster scores high on collectivism in family relationships, and is high-context when it comes to communication.

Things to consider:

The importance of expressive greetings as well as communal and matriarchal ways of organising life.

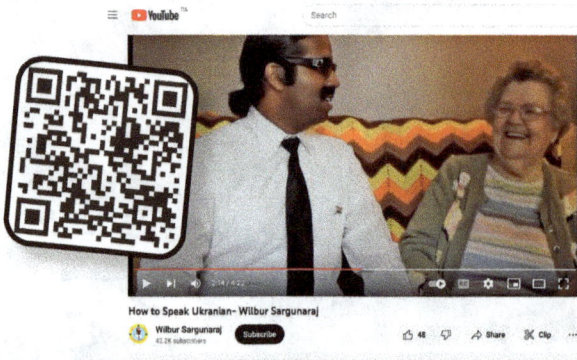

How to Speak Ukranian- Wilbur Sargunaraj
Wilbur Sargunaraj

With Abdul at Odeon of Herodes. Acropolis, Athens, Greece

GERMANIC EUROPE

Germany, the Netherlands, German-speaking Switzerland, Austria and other countries.

Germanic languages bring this cluster of countries together, and they share a lot of common history. Countries in this cluster are very individualistic, and prefer a low-context communication style, being very direct. Countries like Germany are highly competitive, which makes them a 'doing'-oriented culture. An outlier here would be the Netherlands, which has more of a 'being' orientation. Time-orientation in this cluster is monochronic; being punctual, and adhering to structured schedules is important.

Things to consider:

The importance of punctuality, the practice of low power distance, and high regard for academics.

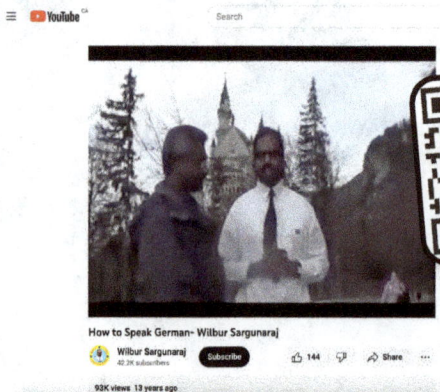

How to Speak German- Wilbur Sargunaraj
Wilbur Sargunaraj
42.3K subscribers
Subscribe
144
Share
93K views 13 years ago

Tompouce in Bleskensgraaf, Netherlands

LATIN EUROPE

Italy, France, Spain, Portugal and other countries.

A love for food, being expressive, and the Romance languages, are things that unite this cluster. The Latin Europe cluster is affective; people are often animated, and use physical gestures for communication and to express themselves. The Catholic Church plays an important role in this cluster, and there is a dislike for uncertainty, with many people adhering to religious and social norms. This cluster tends to be more orientated towards 'being' over 'doing', and this is seen in countries like Italy and France where extended food and coffee breaks to socialize are enjoyed.

Things to consider:

The importance of dining, the distinction between work and family, and valuing tradition.

How to tie the tie: Wilbur Sargunaraj in Paris

Vannakam and Bonjour!
Paris, France

ANGLO

United States, Canada, Australia, the United Kingdom, New Zealand, and other countries.

While the Anglo cluster is scattered geographically, the English language and a colonial history are shared between the countries. Countries in the Anglo cluster can be extremely individualistic and independent, placing a huge emphasis on personal and individual rights. This is a 'doing'-oriented cluster, in which very low-context communication is normal. An interesting addition to this cluster is the Afrikaans-speaking white community in South Africa, which also has its roots in colonization.

Things to consider:

The importance of punctuality, giving people a lot of personal space, and respecting personal rights.

Swansea punk rock band, KD
Knows My Name,
London, United Kingdom

LATIN AMERICA

Brazil, Colombia, Mexico, Venezuela, and other countries.

Cultures in the Latin American cluster are 'being'-oriented, and place significant importance on the enjoyment and quality of life. Countries here are especially people-oriented, and family and friends are held with the utmost importance. The Latin American cluster is very affective, with expressive communication and a small sense of space. Time in this cluster is very fluid, and more attention is given to relationships than to rigid work schedules. Most people in this cluster speak Spanish, with the notable exception of Brazil where Portuguese is the dominant language, and more cultural distinctions exist compared to the rest of the cluster.

Things to consider:

The importance of expressive communication, people having a small sense of personal space, and family above work.

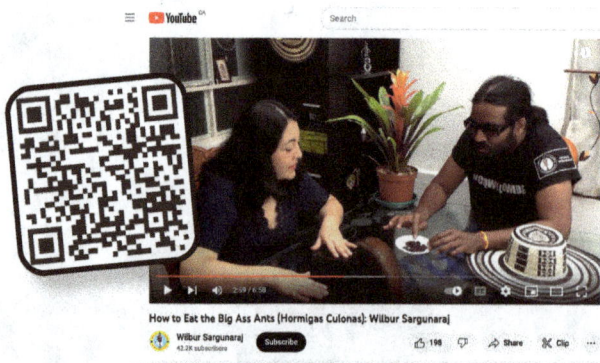

How to Eat the Big Ass Ants (Hormigas Culonas): Wilbur Sargunaraj

Making music together!
Bogota, Colombia

INDIGENOUS

Cultures and peoples like the Māori, Inuit, Hawaiian, Aboriginal, and Torres Strait Islanders.

Most of the Indigenous cultures in this cluster share a history of colonization. Many Indigenous peoples maintain their own sense of identity and values, and hold them distinct from the dominant culture of the cluster where they reside. The territory of Nunavut is the homeland of the Inuit, and they have been able to establish their own governing system within Canada. Hawaii would also be a good example of a place and people who have a distinct Indigenous culture, yet reside within the Anglo cluster. The importance of ohana (family) in the Hawaiian culture, and whānau (extended family) and whakapapa (genealogy) in the Māori culture, point to the fact that the Indigenous cluster is highly collectivist. Groups within the Indigenous cluster often share cooperative values, with an emphasis on working together as part of the tribe, clan, or group. Indigenous cultures generally have a strong connection to the land, and hold community elders in high regard.

Things to consider:

The importance of self-determination as a people, connection to the land, and respect for elders.

A Guide to the Pōwhiri Ceremony in Aotearoa, New Zealand. Featuring Dr. Pouroto Ngaropo.

Reconcili-ACTION,
Treaty 6 Territory,
Turtle Island, Canada

CULTURAL APPRECIATION OR APPROPRIATION?

Is it wrong to wear traditional clothing from other cultures? What about getting a tattoo with Indigenous or cultural symbols? Who can play music that is from a specific culture? Cultural exchange and appreciation can be meaningful and enriching. Cultural appropriation refers to the adoption or use of elements from one culture by members of another culture without consulting, understanding, receiving permission, or respecting the significance of those elements. Cultural appropriation can also perpetuate stereotypes and erode the original culture's identity. Are you approaching cultural exchange with a willingness and sensitivity to learn about and honour the origins of the cultural elements? The difference between cultural appreciation and appropriation often hinges on whether there is a respectful acknowledgment of the cultural context involved.

CHAPTER 5
Unconscious Bias

"No one is born hating another person because of the color of his skin, or his background, or his religion. People must learn to hate, and if they can learn to hate, they can be taught to love, for love comes more naturally to the human heart than its opposite."

Nelson Mandela

Now that we have looked at the cultural values and clusters, it's important to remind ourselves once again to avoid generalizations and stereotypes. Not all Japanese people will be high-context communicators, not all Kenyans will adopt a polychronic approach to time, and the list goes on. This is important because if we relate to people only using stereotypes, we will deepen our own unconscious bias.

So, what is unconscious bias? Bias is a tendency to favor one thing over another, and it is important to realize that everyone has bias, and that our biases are sometimes unconscious. These hidden biases can be based on inaccurate stereotypes that have been learned indirectly from our family, our friends, the institutions that we're part of, and the media we consume. The term "stereotype" originated in the printing industry, where it referred to a kind of plate or mold used for producing multiple fixed copies of a particular page or design. As time progressed, the term was metaphorically used to describe a fixed and over simplified idea or belief regarding a specific group of individuals.

Stereotypes can also be formed through our interactions with others. Biases can be developed on the basis of gender, skin colour, accents, or even a person's name – I can give you countless of examples of being profiled or stereotyped because of my accent, the name 'Sargunaraj', or my dark skin! Sadly, I have also had to confront my own racism and prejudice as I have caught myself stereotyping people at different times and in different places. Stereotypes influence how we interact with people – what we think of them, and what we expect of them. Left unchecked, our unconscious bias can lead to prejudice, discrimination, ethnocentrism, and racism.

One of the most important steps for combating racism is admitting and acknowledging that we have hidden bias. When we do this, it helps us to avoid thinking with generalizations, to slow down, and to try and stop ourselves from stereotyping the people we're interacting with.

Beyond this, an important way to avoid using stereotypes is to focus on the characteristics of individuals rather than the identity of the larger group which we think they are part of. This means taking the time to develop personal relationships with people and listen to individual perspectives. Taking these steps will lead you on the road to becoming a culturally intelligent citizen!

BREAKING DOWN STEREOTYPES

Positive stereotypes may seem complimentary on the surface but they can be oversimplified views and overlook the uniqueness of individuals (e.g. Canadians are polite and friendly). Negative stereotypes convey harmful assumptions about a particular group which reinforces prejudice (e.g. Americans are loud and obsessed with guns). In both cases, whether positive or negative, stereotypes contribute to misunderstanding, bias, and inaccurate beliefs about specific groups of people. When you meet someone from a different culture, try to look beyond stereotypes to determine your response. Develop personal relationships with people and listen to individual perspectives.

ADDRESSING BIAS – A PERSONAL STORY

I'll never forget the time when I was walking my dog down the streets of Madurai and stopped at our small outdoor corner shop to pick up groceries for my Amma. In front of the shop there were two men who I would have described as 'African'. (At that time, I didn't realize that there were many countries within Africa!) I was around ten years old and excited as this was my first encounter with someone from the continent! The two men smiled at me, beckoned my dog to come and just as they started to pet it, one of the men gave a swift kick to my dog's stomach. My dog yelped, while the two men laughed and walked away. I was shocked and furious. I wondered what kind of people do these things, and whether everyone from Africa behaved this way.

During my college days I had the opportunity to play professionally with a Congolese band. While I enjoyed their music and friendship, they sometimes failed to pay me as agreed. In another incident, a Ugandan acquaintance promised he had arranged room and board for me when I was moving to a new city. After numerous phone calls and much stress, I found out that he had lied and I was left to figure things out on my own (thankfully, a loving family I had recently met welcomed me into their home)! I must confess that due to these experiences, my upbringing, and the portrayal of Africans by some media, I held a bias against anyone from the continent for a while. I harboured the misguided belief that they were all out to take advantage of me.

Although I did meet wonderful people from African countries, I always held them at a distance. I convinced myself that I was not prejudiced and believed that I was good at making friends from around the world. Over time, I started to realize that I had an issue that needed to be dealt with as I didn't want to harbour bitterness and mistrust.

I decided that the first step would be to acknowledge that I had a bias which needed to be confronted. When I started traveling for work in Africa, I met incredible people whose generosity, hospitality, and friendship helped me to deal with this. What I had needed was to enter into deeper relationships with people and get to know their perspectives. I will admit, this wasn't easy as I had to be vulnerable and take the risk of opening myself to others.

Listening to stories, asking questions, and practising empathy were all part of the journey in helping me deal with my bias. Not everyone from the continent was out to hurt or cheat me! Because of these encounters I now have some amazing friends from Kenya, Uganda, Democratic Republic of Congo, Rwanda, and other countries across the beautiful continent of Africa. These friends remind me of what happens when we break down our walls, confront our bias, and enter into the world of our 'other'.

Dealing with my bias helped pave the way for newfound friendships and opened doors for honest discussions. This

UNCONSCIOUS BIAS

Unconscious bias occurs when we automatically and unintentionally rely on stereotypes or preconceptions without realizing it. These biases impact how we understand things, make decisions, and act. Hidden biases can be based on inaccurate stereotypes that have been learned indirectly through family, friends, institutions, and the media, and these stereotypes can also be formed through our interactions with others. Unconscious bias affects everyone and no individual is immune as these biases are deeply ingrained in the fabric of our society and culture. Are you willing to be humble, making an effort to recognize and address any biases you may have?

Making new friends
at the *Exploring CQ*
event in Beijing, China

also helped me practise empathy and become aware of what some of my African friends were experiencing in India and other parts of the world. Many Africans come to India for education and employment opportunities, only to be disheartened by the extent of discrimination they encounter. Sadly, this racism and Afrophobia is a recurring, widespread issue in Indian society, fuelled by inaccurate stereotypes. For example, India's cinema industry often has negative portrayals of Africans as drug dealers and criminals and these racist stereotypes fuel hatred and incite violence. The occurrence of violent attacks and abuse against African students studying in India has been particularly alarming.

A few years ago, I had the opportunity to work with the **黑是美** *(Black is Beautiful)* campaign in Beijing where we documented stories of African university students facing racial discrimination. Like India, many blacks in China are on the receiving end of disparaging comments; they are sometimes refused housing because of the colour of their skin and are considered inferior. This is a stark reminder of how important it is for every person to confront their bias, and not allow stereotypes to shape their views of people who are different from them. If we refuse to address this, we will continue to reinforce the system of racism that says all people are not equal and that subordination to a 'superior' race is normal.

While I have shared these observations, obviously not all Chinese or Indians hold prejudiced views towards others. I

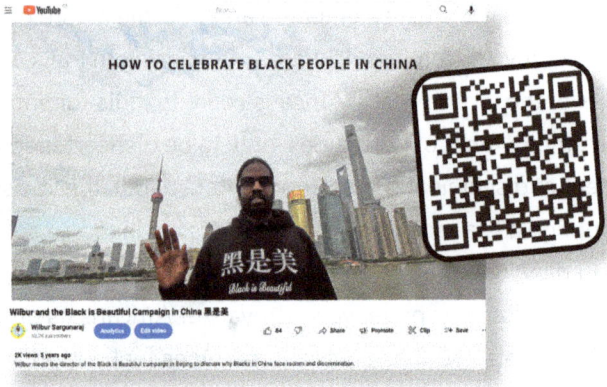

know many individuals from these communities who are actively working to break down barriers of discrimination, challenge stereotypes, and promote inclusivity and understanding.

FEAR OF THE 'OTHER'

The 'other' is a term used to describe how we respond to someone else when we view or treat them as intrinsically different from ourselves, whether ethnically, geographically, economically, ideologically, or otherwise. The concept of the 'other' involves individuals establishing two clear-cut categories: an 'us', encompassing those who belong to their group or identity, and a 'them', consisting of individuals perceived as outsiders or different.

I experienced 'othering' during my childhood when my relatives and family introduced me to the concept of caste, and taught me about this social classification which makes clear distinctions between people in India. Talking about caste was taboo, and my family always whispered when the subject was brought up. I found this very confusing as a young boy. I was taught to look at certain people differently; they had the same skin colour and we spoke the same language, yet I was supposed to avoid them. In addition, I wasn't supposed to let anyone know what caste I belonged to!

What confused me even more was the fact that we would hear sermons about how all people are equal in God's eyes. Yet, as some Christians walked out of the church doors after the service, they would exclude and discriminate on the basis of caste. We would voice the national pledge every morning at school that 'all Indians are my brothers and sisters' yet continue to treat fellow Indians as outcasts. It just didn't make sense!

When you meet someone from Tamil Nadu, they will often ask you the question, "Yenthe ooru?" which means, "Where are you from?" or more accurately, "What's your native place?". At the root of the question, there can be a desire to size you up and find out what caste you belong to, in order to determine where you fit in the power hierarchy.

Growing up I saw the unrelenting oppression and humiliation of 'low caste' people in my village. Fights and clashes between different castes over property and resources were common. I even remember reading horrible stories in the newspaper about young lovers from different castes committing suicide or being murdered because their families would not allow them to be together.

It was during this time that I was introduced to another form of discrimination in India. *Shadeism* or *colourism* is a form of prejudice in which people are treated differently based on the shade of their skin. When a baby is born, relatives ask questions about how fair the child is, and the shade of skin between siblings is frequently compared. Along with millions of other Indian children I was told to never stand in the sun because it would make me darker and undesirable. The idea of being 'fair and lovely' was pushed by relatives, advertisements, movies, and society around me. I was consistently reminded that people like me, belonging to a specific caste and possessing dark skin had less value and were considered inherently unattractive. The discriminatory view that dark is ugly, while fair is lovely, persists in Indian society and remains prevalent in many parts of the world.

I eventually realized that I did not have to give power to the concept of caste. I chose not to internalize society's messages that portrayed dark skin as being undesirable. I needed to start believing in the truth that my self-worth and success come from knowing that I am beautiful and valuable just the way I am. Instead of seeing external categories created by society

DARK IS BEAUTIFUL

There is a connection between colourism, caste, and colonialism: being fair meant you were seen as superior, while being darker meant you were lower on the social hierarchy ladder. In many countries across Africa, Asia, and South America, a remnant of the colonial mentality appears in the preference for lighter skin tones. People have unconsciously associated shades of skin with power and status, and applied this to the members of their own group. This is why a massive market for toxic skin-whitening products exists. The companies that market these products keep inflicting damage to the self-worth of countless people by spreading the lie that the value and beauty of people is determined by the shade of their skin. Campaigns in India like *Dark is Beautiful*, draw attention to the effects of skin-colour bias and celebrate the beauty and diversity of all skin tones. Dark is beautiful, fair is beautiful, everyone is beautiful just the way we are!

BuzzFeed

This Music Video Hilariously Explains Why We All Need To Get Over The Colour Of Our Skin

Wilbur's New Video Sends A Message: 'I'm Very Dark And Proud Of It'

THE TIMES OF INDIA

Chennai Times

Being fair is not a prerequisite to being successful: Wilbur

that divide and marginalize, I have been on a lifelong journey of learning to focus on the beauty of each human being and all that unites us.

Another example of being taught to see some people as the 'other' was how I learned to view people from Pakistan. I had never met anyone from Pakistan, but I grew up believing they were my enemies because I would hear this from my family, my friends, and the media.

Unfortunately, this is true for people across both nations. India and Pakistan have had a historically tumultuous political relationship, and you can see this being played out in the sport of cricket as well – talk to anyone who follows the sport and they will tell you one of the biggest rivalries on the pitch is between India and Pakistan, two cricket-crazy countries! This is not just a friendly rivalry. The burning of effigies, attacks on players, and violent fan clashes, are among the reasons why the two teams historically could not play the sport together on their own soil.

When I left India, I finally met people from Pakistan, and they were nothing like what I had imagined them to be. We could eat together, laugh together, and of course watch cricket together – I didn't have to fear them as I had been taught by the society I grew up in! It has been so encouraging to see recent efforts in cricket diplomacy, where the two countries have played the occasional game in India or in Pakistan. While tensions remain high, hopefully taking the step of sitting together for a one-day (or five-day) game in a stadium is a starting point to break down some of this fear.

It's so important that we deal with our fear of the strange and unknown. The cure for 'othering' is to gain more understanding of the people we find different and to start engaging with them so we can see their humanity. Recently I was at Auschwitz and had time to reflect on one of the most terrible atrocities in history. What started off with fear and hatred of the 'other' ended with genocide. Genocide doesn't begin with gas chambers or when we lift a gun or machete. It begins when we fear one another.

My friend Carl Wilkens is an inspiring human being who stayed in Rwanda during the 1994 genocide and saved the lives of numerous people. I remember him saying once that, "the seeds of genocide are planted when I begin to say that my world would be better if you were not in it." These seeds are planted when people teach that caste or race are justified ways to value people. These seeds are planted when we perceive those from other countries or communities as our enemies, as inferior to us, or as dangerous. When we stop seeing someone as human, it becomes easy to diminish their worth and value. This was especially evident during the Rwandan genocide when referring to individuals as 'cockroaches' was one way to justify the mass killings. We continue to observe similar dehumanizing tactics in other conflicts around the world.

I recently had a conversation with Sally Azar, one of the first Palestinian women to be ordained as a pastor in the Holy Land. She described how Israelis and Palestinians can come together despite the years of violence and hatred. "In this part of the world there is so much that separates us. The most obvious example is the wall that separates Israeli and Palestinian land, but we see this separation played out every day, from schools to transportation, neighbourhoods, and much more. This physical wall unfortunately becomes a spiritual wall in people's hearts and minds."

In order for these walls to break, Sally believes that there needs to be more communication, and more places in which people can encounter the 'other'. There should be more opportunities created for both parties to come together to address issues of identity, history, and what prevents reconciliation. I think the most important thing I took away from our conversation was that we need to see each other as human beings before we see them as anything else.

"Suffering and pain is an everyday experience for many in this region, and having empathy for people who are hurting, regardless of their race or religion, is extremely important." In order for reconciliation and peace to happen, the walls we have built in our countries and in our hearts need to be broken down, and trust needs to be restored.

Fear of the 'other' leads us down the path of prejudice and judgment, and keeps us insular, isolated within our own tribe and culture. Fear keeps us from encountering people who are not like us, and keeps us from discovering that the other person is human, and that they are beautiful.

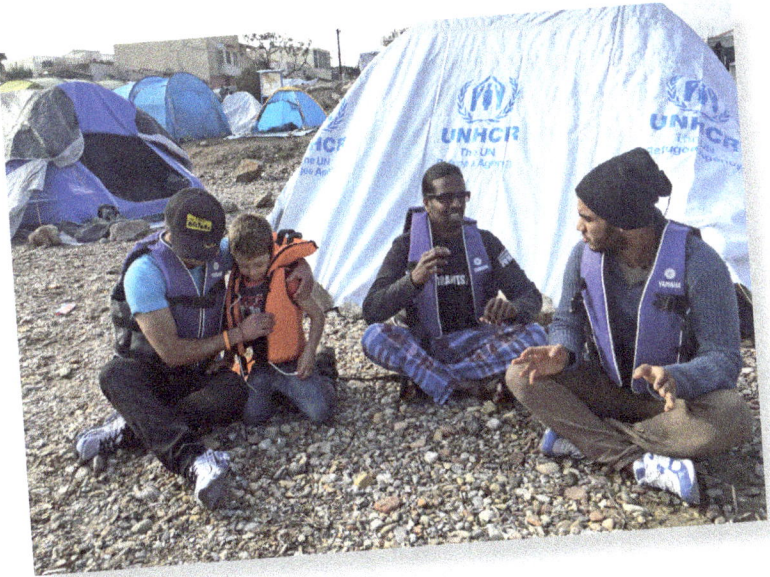

FEAR OF THE OTHER

Something beautiful happens when we enter into the world of our perceived 'other'. Differences cease to scare us as we start to dialogue and as we learn from each other's perspectives. We may not share the same opinions or values, but something extraordinary takes place when we confront our bias and get to know one another.

FROM FEAR TO FRIENDS

It was a four-hour journey from Kampala to Kasensero. I was in Uganda and would have plenty of time to contemplate my unjustified fear of meeting people from Africa. I was partnering with an organization that worked with migrants and we were heading into the heart of the country to document their stories. All along the way I was secretly building more walls to protect myself. I made a plan to conduct the interviews, then turn around and leave as soon as possible so I could keep interactions to a minimum.

We pulled up to the tiny fishing village of Kasensero, where we met with the project coordinator. She took the videographer and me through a winding maze of tiny shacks with corrugated tin roofs. The deeper we went into this impoverished place the more uncomfortable I felt.

Along the way there were friendly adults and children saying hello with beautiful smiles, but because of my deep seated bias, I found it challenging to trust anyone. All I could think of was protecting my equipment. The last time I was in Africa, my iPod had been stolen while I was riding in a matatu (mini bus) – so there was fear in me, and there was prejudice, and there was judgment. I badly wanted to conduct the interview back by the main road where I felt safe and comfortable.

After a ten-minute walk, we were introduced to a lady named Irene. Irene was a sex worker and peer educator for several young girls involved in this profession in Kasensero. With her young son by her side, Irene warmly introduced herself and welcomed us into her simple home. It was a single room with space only for the cot she used for work, so we sat on the living room floor.

Eager to finish the interview quickly, I dove straight in and asked if we could start. Irene, unaware of my unease, burst into a huge smile and said that she was so excited to host someone from India! She started talking about her love for Indian music and cinema, and exclaimed how she wanted to wear a sari and be part of a Bollywood music video. She opened up a small box and showed me photographs of when she was in high school and explained how she loved being on her school drama team.

As Irene shared more of her life story and how she had ended up in Kasensero, I began to let my guard down. She spoke about the hardships of being a single mother, and the awful situations she found herself in. I listened closely, realizing there was a growing sense of empathy within me as she helped me to see things from her perspective. Irene was genuine, vulnerable and there was something different about this encounter. I wasn't meeting someone from Uganda or Africa but I was making a deep connection with a fellow human being!

I didn't have to be scared of Irene. Fear of the 'other' had kept me from forming relationships with people from Africa in the past, but now this fear was replaced by a genuine thirst for meaningful friendship as I confronted my bias in Irene's little house. This was an encounter that would change the way I would interact with people from various countries in Africa, and the change in me happened not by attending a corporate diversity and inclusion workshop, but by listening to a sex worker in a tiny fishing village in Uganda.

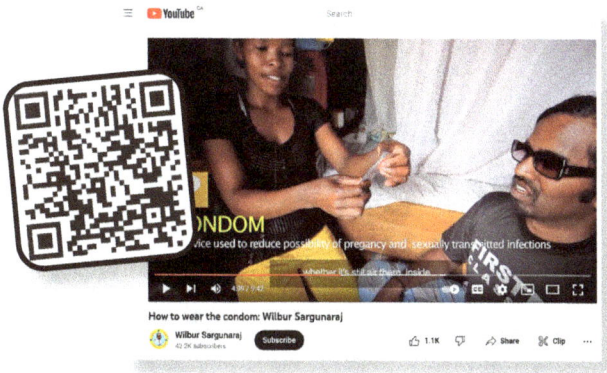

How to wear the condom: Wilbur Sargunaraj

Something divine took place on that day, and as we parted ways, I promised Irene that I would be back! I may not be a Bollywood star with connections to get her on the big screen, but I knew I certainly could find her a sari!

Fast forward two years to when I partnered with a local organization in Kasensero called CIPA (Community Intervention for the prevention of HIV AIDS). We were excited to work together to empower women like Irene and help them with options to exit the sex trade if they chose. My friend Nitinkumar who owns a garment shop in Bangalore heard that I was returning to see Irene, and gifted her a beautiful silk sari.

Sari in hand, I went with CIPA to find Irene. I was welcomed again by that same beautiful smile, and as we hugged each other I thanked her again for what she did to transform my life. I presented her the sari, and then told her I had one more gift!

I had written a song for her, and was hoping to film the music video with Irene and her friends who were also sex workers. The song was called 'End the Sex Trade', and dressed in her sari, Irene, along with her friends and I, had an incredible day filming, laughing and eating together. Irene may not have been a Bollywood star, but she definitely was a 'simple superstar'. As we wrapped up filming in this Ugandan fishing village, I was reminded that something extraordinary can happen when we overcome fear and move towards being friends!

Wilbur Sargunaraj: Vazhapazham Matoke - Official Music Video

Wilbur Sargunaraj
47.2K subscribers

Subscribe

137

WHY CAN'T WE BE COLOUR BLIND?

People who claim that they are colour blind or believe that they treat all people equally need to be cautious. Being colour blind is a nice idea but it takes away characteristics of a person's identity by not recognizing their colour, race, or culture – it's better to share our cultures and experiences than pretend they're not there.

CHAPTER 6

Reconcili-Action

> "Achieving reconciliation is like climbing a mountain — we must proceed a step at a time. It will not always be easy. There will be storms, there will be obstacles, but we cannot allow ourselves to be daunted by the task because our goal is just and it is also necessary. Remember, reconciliation is yours to achieve."
>
> **Murray Sinclair,**
> *Former Senator and Chairman of the Truth and Reconciliation Commission, Canada*

At the beginning of the book, I shared how I developed a bias towards Indigenous people when I first arrived in Canada. I believed the negative stereotypes I took on from the world around me, and they moved me further away from developing relationships. It wouldn't be right if I were to work on overcoming bias with people who live in other parts of the world, but not work to build positive relationships with Indigenous neighbours right in my community.

While Canada is known for generally having a progressive stance
of welcoming refugees and immigrants, what some people
may not know is that Canada has a dire race problem. Having
lived in a number of Canadian provinces, I have seen first-hand
that there is a stark and noticeable line that divides Settler and
Indigenous communities. On Treaty 6 Territory in Saskatchewan,
I have seen this racism fuel a harmful 'them' and 'us' mentality,
and I could share numerous stories of my Indigenous friends who
have experienced discrimination. Since I live on Treaty 6 territory,
working towards reconciliation with the first people who lived on
this land is an extremely important part of the work I do.

Truth and Reconciliation commissions have been established
in countries including Canada, Australia, South Africa, and New
Zealand to provide opportunities for Indigenous people to share
their past experiences and stories. These commissions work
to uncover the truth and reveal past injustices in the hope that
people can heal and work towards reconciliation.

Reconciliation essentially means making peace after conflict or
restoring a relationship that has been broken. Reconciliation has
become a familiar word, but it is difficult for individuals to know
how to make reconciliation a reality. My personal journey to
reconciliation began by first acknowledging that I had a bias. I
then began educating myself on our shared history and actively
sought to enter into relationships with Indigenous people in my
community. I read books, took classes, attended Indigenous

events, and met with Indigenous leaders to help me decolonize my thinking. Using my platform as a musician and consultant, I started partnering with Indigenous educators and co-presenting with them at schools, concerts, and events to show what genuine reconciliation could look like.

RECONCILIATION AND CULTURAL INTELLIGENCE

As I have taken my *Exploring CQ* event across Canada, I developed a way to help my audience and I remember how to take specific steps towards reconciliation.   Since Canadians are known for using the word 'eh', let's use a play on this word! Here are the four A's (or 'Eh's') of reconciliation:

- Gain AWARENESS of Indigenous and colonial history

- ACKNOWLEDGE the injustices of past and present

- Be willing to make AMENDS where you can

- Take ACTION to change behaviour

The ideas behind the four 'A's' of reconciliation will be familiar to you by now – they are rooted in the four capabilities of cultural intelligence. Reconciliation is hard work, but everyone can do it, and I want to share how these capabilities can be used to reconcile relationships between Indigenous and Non-Indigenous people. These ideas can also be applied in other contexts where relationships are strained or have been broken. I have approached this from my perspective as a Settler in Canada.

CQ DRIVE: *Develop your interest in connecting with Indigenous people.* Certain individuals follow protocols and acknowledge treaties, but find it difficult to actually get to know their Indigenous neighbours. You can take action by confronting your bias and asking yourself what is stopping you from taking steps towards meaningful interactions. If you find this challenging, start small by attending cultural ceremonies, finding Indigenous music and art, or sampling food at local Indigenous restaurants, and slowly progress towards deeper interaction. There will be challenges and frustrations, but persevering is part of practising CQ Drive.

CQ KNOWLEDGE: *Educate yourself on shared history.* In a country like Canada, increasing your CQ Knowledge means learning about many things, including residential schools, the Indian Act, Missing and Murdered Indigenous Women (MMIW), and the impact that assimilation policies have had on Indigenous people. Acknowledging history, especially the injustices that have occurred, is very important. Some non-Indigenous people brush off history by saying, "It happened in the past, can't they just move on?" or "I wasn't there, it wasn't my fault". Acknowledging the injustices of the past and the present-day impact from them takes humility and is necessary for the ongoing work of reconciliation. How have you benefited from systems that have oppressed Indigenous peoples?

CQ STRATEGY: *Ask the Question 'Why'.* Instead of being quick to judge, can you take the time to analyze the attitudes and prejudices that hold you back from making connections? Here's an example. I have had conversations with people who have casually used the phrase "drunken Indian", stereotyping Indigenous people as 'drunks'. This racist language is unfair, untrue, and compounds the discrimination which Indigenous people experience. While there are some Indigenous people who struggle with addictions, it is important to ask the question 'Why?'. Reasons for this are well documented and include intergenerational trauma, the horror of residential schools, the ongoing experience of racism, and the impacts of colonialism.

Using cultural intelligence can help to stop us from stereotyping and can enable us to see perspectives we may not have seen before, which are more in line with reality.

CQ ACTION: *Change your behaviour.* Reconciliation means coming together, fixing what has been broken, and working towards healing. We can choose to stay on our side of town and to hold on to our biases, or we can be active in developing deeper relationships. Appropriately adjusting your behaviour (both non-verbal and verbal), and adapting your communication style are both important when you are trying to develop these new connections.

Learning a few key phrases and understanding protocols are all part of cultural intelligence action. But more importantly than this, a change of heart is needed in the way we think, feel, and behave. After admitting how our hearts and actions need to change, we can listen with deeper humility to the stories of Indigenous people. Truth and openness are foundational to the reconciliation process and necessary to move toward forgiveness and healing.

As we discussed in Chapter One, cultural intelligence is your ability to function and relate effectively with people from different cultures. Part of relating and functioning as human beings means that we are bound to encounter tensions and brokenness in our relationships. Being aware of the past, acknowledging wrongdoing, making amends, and taking action are all part of reconciliation. Governments and institutions have a role to play in this, but they cannot change the hearts of individuals. It is up to you and me to enter into relationship and make reconciliation a reality!

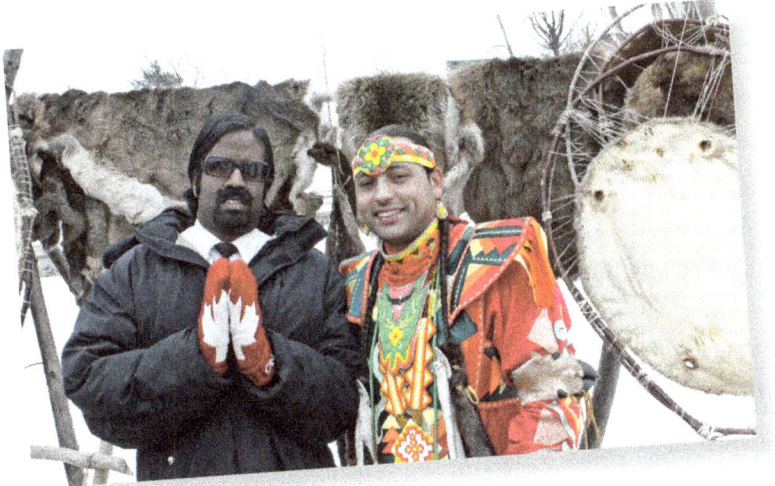

RECONCILI-ACTION

I had the amazing opportunity to participate in an inspiring event known as the Spruce River Folk Festival. This annual event takes place on Treaty 6 Territory in Saskatchewan, Canada, where a Mennonite community and the Young Chippeweyan (Stony Knoll) First Nation come together in the spirit of reconciliation and peace.

The two communities come together to discuss how they can solve issues which have arisen since First Nations' reserve land was given over to the Mennonite communities back in the 19th century. There is food, music, dance, and storytelling, and reconciliation can be tangibly seen as the Settler community actively takes steps to right the wrongs of the past by giving back land to the First Nation communities.

Being part of this festival showed me how important taking action is in reconciliation! The work of reconciliation can be hard for both parties, especially as Indigenous people are dealing with trauma. It's so important to persevere and to approach relationships with an attitude of learning and humility. Like the Young Chippeweyan First Nation and the Mennonite community, make it a priority to come together side by side and learn from each other so that you can work towards reconciliation and healing.

What is Orange Shirt Day? Bob Joseph- Indigenous Master Trainer
Wilbur Sargunaraj

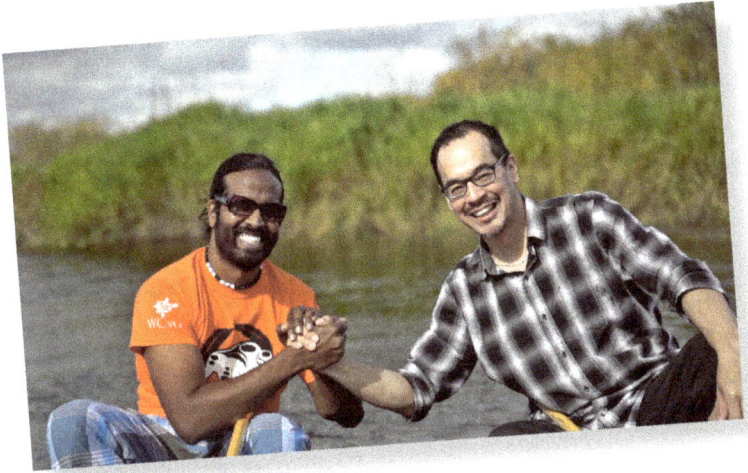

THE TWO ROW WAMPUM

Whenever I hear a treaty acknowledgement in Canada or read about treaties from other nations, I am reminded of an agreement that captures the spirit of coming together with all our differences and living together in harmony. While other treaties have been made over the years between Indigenous and Settlers, the Guswentha Treaty of 1613 stands out for me.

Also known as the Two Row Wampum (belt), it is a beautiful commitment to peace and friendship between two completely different cultures. It is one of the first treaties, and it was made between the Haudenosaunee (Iroquois) and the Dutch who came to settle on Turtle Island (North America) in the 1600s.

Initially, the Dutch proposed a very patriarchal relationship which would see them as fathers and the Haudenosaunee people as their children. The Haudenosaunee people were not fond of this approach, and proposed instead that they would not be like father and son, but like brothers.

The two purple rows on the wampum symbolize two canoes or paths, traveling together in the same direction. One canoe represented the Indigenous people, and the other canoe represented the Dutch Settlers. Neither party would steer each other's canoe, telling them what to do, but instead they would move together, side by side. The three rows of white beads symbolize 'peace', 'friendship', and 'forever'.

This agreement was founded on the existence together of two distinct nations. As I shared earlier from my story in Iqaluit, reconciliation is not a simple process, but a lifelong journey of listening, learning, and adapting. It is more than just a buzz word that gets thrown around a few times a year. As we keep an open mind, understand different perspectives, and treat all people equitably, we will be able to row side by side as the treaty says, *"as long as the grass is green, as long as the rivers flow downhill and as long as the sun rises in the east and sets in the west".*

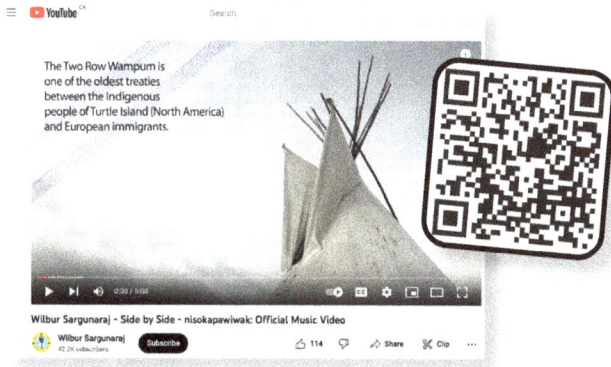

The Two Row Wampum is one of the oldest treaties between the Indigenous people of Turtle Island (North America) and European immigrants.

Wilbur Sargunaraj – Side by Side - nisokapawiwak: Official Music Video

Wilbur Sargunaraj
42.2K subscribers

Subscribe

114

Share   Clip   ...

RECONCILIATION AROUND OUR WORLD

I want to conclude this chapter with a collection of thoughts on reconciliation. I have had the honour of working with friends from around the world who are making a difference in their communities. I asked them to share a few thoughts on how they view reconciliation in their local contexts.

AUSTRALIA

For genuine reconciliation to happen, a cultural paradigm shift is needed – a new lens to help us look past the biases of traditions built on ignorance and pride. In Australia that lens is currently being called 'truth telling,' and it is fundamental for us if we want to move forward. It's hard to build for a better future without first acknowledging the problems that have preceded us. Understanding that the very real injustices of the past inform intergenerational trauma and disadvantage in the present will better equip us to address these issues and achieve actual growth.

The most obvious step toward this outcome is the mammoth task of overhauling how Australian history is taught by the Australian government's education system. A more practical step for an individual waiting for the colonial structure around them to change is to read books by Aboriginal authors and have actual conversations with people who hold relevant lived experience. For those wondering how to approach that, my advice is to get out to Aboriginal community events and meet some people. A great place to start is NAIDOC Week. It was initially a single day (as the history of the acronym would show —National Aborigines and Islanders Day Observance Committee) but now, the celebrations last a week to a month. NAIDOC week with its wide range of events is a great way to begin the journey of reconciliation.

Shannon 'monks' Smith
Artist, Workshop Designer and Facilitator
Gomeroi Clan, Kamilaroi Nation (Australia)

GREENLAND

As a teacher of Greenlandic language, I have seen many cases where the willingness to try to speak the Greenlandic language has created a lot of trust and respect. As a heritage of the colonial past, the Danish language has been the language of prestige and power here – and furthermore, it has been the language necessary when you wanted an education. All of this makes equality of languages so important. In the case of the Greenlandic language, it is admittedly somewhat harder to learn than English, German, or other related languages. That's why it is crucial to accept that perfection is nice but completely unnecessary in order to relate heart to heart. In my opinion it is very important to forget about perfection and enter a new world of the funny exchange of sounds! Danish or Inuit people should not be afraid to make mistakes! The goal is to connect with people heart to heart! Every time I see people bonding and connecting with each other is when they have a childish, playful, and trustful approach to the world. In my experience, the bonds that are formed this way are the strongest and the most heartfelt. In this way, reconciliation will be seen as we create beautiful new connections as equals.

Aviaja Becky Larson
Kalaallisut Language Instructor
Kalaalit Nunaat, Greenland

HAWAII

As a Hawaiian it has always been my goal in life to spread Aloha. But how do you show Aloha when you're dealing with settlers, colonization, and your land being taken over? In Hawaii there are many locals that have lost this sense of Aloha and are living in anger and resentment. I can't change the past and what has happened, so I have made it a point to develop relationships with people from all around the world who come to my land. Using my platform as a chef, I am now using food as a way to make friends and educate tourists so that they can start to look beyond the resorts and the beaches, and connect with us locals. It has been hard, as I find myself being frustrated with how Hawaii has been romanticized while locals cannot even afford to live on their own land and are forced to leave for the mainland. I could remain angry, but I know that will not lead to good. My goal remains to keep spreading Aloha and unite people of all backgrounds in the land that I love. This reconciliation is possible when we let go of bitterness and hurt, and work towards fixing these broken relationships in Aloha!

Shadd Naleieha
Culinarian
Maui, Hawaii

CANADA

Although I never personally attended a residential school, I'm affected by the inter-generational trauma from the five generations of my family who did. The knowledge and understanding of this trauma is now being spoken of across Canada. Everyone is in a different place on the road to reconciliation. I believe we can have the most impact in working toward reconciliation by being willing to engage with Indigenous peoples in our communities. This can happen more easily when we break stereotypes, stop blaming victims for their situations, and listen to each other's stories in genuine humility. It is important for all Canadians to educate themselves with Indigenous history, and to recognize their privilege and all the ways they have benefited. While it might seem long and arduous, we need to stick to the trail and do everything to make reconciliation a reality!

Darcy Pelletier
Educator
Muscowpetung Saulteaux Nation #80, Treaty 4 Territory,
Turtle Island (Canada)

SOUTH AFRICA

First and foremost, we need to be open-minded, willing to learn, and to acknowledge people's experience and past pains. Starting from that understanding it is easier to get to know each other on a personal level. We need to acknowledge that we are all different and unique, and that our diversity is what is worth celebrating. In South Africa we may be living in a free and democratic society, but we need to acknowledge the fact that we still carry baggage from the apartheid era. This has put each of us at different places, and the need to level the playing field for all is critical if we are going to build an inclusive society. Once we build inclusive spaces that allow for honest and critical conversations, which can help us to understand each other, we will be well underway in the quest for reconciliation. We need to learn how to show respect for each other, and how to converse as equals, being open to being called out, and calling out discriminatory behavior. My role working at a white-dominated school as an anti-racism consultant has given me the opportunity to see that reconciliation is possible when we take these small steps together to build an inclusive society.

Busisiwe Nkosi
Zulu, Diversity and Inclusions Specialist
Johannesburg, South Africa

RWANDA

Some might think that reconciliation in Rwanda might not be possible especially after the devastating genocide that took place in 1994. While there was much economic disparity between the Hutu and Tutsi, so much of the hatred was fueled by ethnic animosities, propaganda and manipulation rather than class divisions. Reconciliation not only requires the acknowledgment of wrong but also for allowing the perpetrator to confess and receive forgiveness. In Rwanda having a safe space for dialogue and truth telling has been important, giving the victim and the perpetrator a chance to share their experiences. The community based Gacaca courts have seen great success by blending traditional and modern approaches for justice where perpetrators can seek forgiveness while making amends. Ultimately reconciliation cannot be achieved if truth is not involved. I have always been inspired by individual cases of victims and perpetrators going above and beyond to achieve forgiveness. Imagine a widow forgiving the young murderer of her late husband and children, then choosing to adopt him! Now that is a testament to genuine reconciliation which goes beyond mere justice and reparations!

Jean Robert Kabera
Educator, Kigali, University of Rwanda

AOTEAROA, NEW ZEALAND

Through the process of colonization in Aotearoa (New Zealand), there has been loss of land, hurt, pain, suffering and disconnection on both sides between Māori and Pakeha (white New Zealanders). The process of reconciliation after they have been in a state of discord can be difficult, but this is where we persevere with the power of truth and forgiveness which can create a new path way to living in harmony. Arguments tend to create division and keep us apart from each other which creates a spirit of disunity. It is time to move in a new direction where we take the time to understand each other's hurts. It is time to rise up and to forgive one another for past grievances and claim back our unity as a people with one mind, one heart, one spirit and one universal people. When these new spaces are created, healing will surely come for us here in Aotearoa!

Dr. Pouroto Ngaropō
Tohunga, Historian, Senior Cultural Advisor
Iramoko Marae, Te Tāwera Hapū, Ngāti Awa ki Te Awa o Te Atua, Aotearoa (New Zealand)

CHAPTER 7

Why Cultural Intelligence?

If you are going to be a Culturally Intelligent person, tolerance is aiming too low! Breaking barriers and entering into the world of the 'other' requires a radical transformation of the heart!

Cultural intelligence is valuable both at home and abroad; CQ can help foster reconciliation, develop interpersonal relationships, and it can help organizations be more effective. It is not just an academic concept for travelling business people or jet-setting 'influencers' (certain travel bloggers and 'influencers' on social media could definitely benefit from increasing their CQ)! Instead, cultural intelligence is for all people.

It's clear how CQ would be needed in places where there are large immigrant populations, yet in more culturally homogenous communities which have fewer immigrants, CQ is just as important to allow us to learn from one another. Without CQ, differences in ethnicities, accents, and cultural values can lead to misunderstandings, tensions, and racism. Using cultural intelligence can be the key to open a space where all people can feel welcome, respected, and valued.

It has amazed me how cultural intelligence can be used in almost any context. I have enjoyed working with international companies where the need for effective cross-cultural communication is essential for business. The *Exploring CQ* unconscious bias workshop is an event where people have candid discussions in a safe environment. Witnessing participants take initial steps toward recognizing and addressing their bias has been truly rewarding! In non-profit settings I have worked alongside volunteers who need high CQ to develop trust with the communities in which they are working. I remember the time I was in Chios, Greece, visiting the Souda refugee camp for Syrian refugees. I worked with the NGO Drapen I-Havit from Norway to film an empowering music video called 'Migrants'. This would not have been possible if we hadn't established strong relationships through exercising CQ.

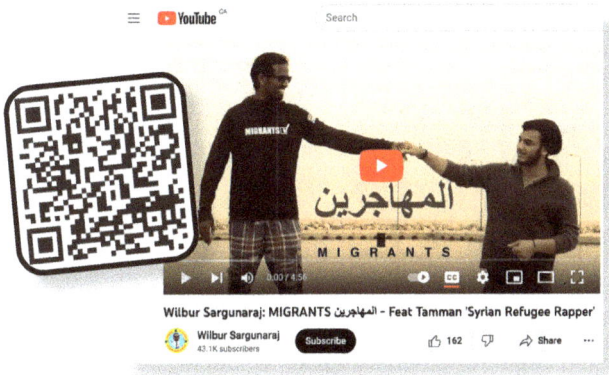

Wilbur Sargunaraj: MIGRANTS المهاجرين – Feat Tamman 'Syrian Refugee Rapper'

Wilbur Sargunaraj
42.1K subscribers

Educational institutions, from elementary schools right through to universities, are all places where CQ is absolutely essential. CQ allows students to feel valued and enables them to experience belonging. Enabling students to become global citizens who appreciate different perspectives is part of how we can lay the foundations of a sustainable society where everyone is able to value each other.

Presenting the *Exploring CQ* workshop at schools is always a rewarding experience. I once spent time at the Francisco Mega High school in Rio de Janeiro, Brazil, where I shared an incredible afternoon of cultural learning exchange. We had meaningful conversations about skin colour bias, discrimination based on socio economic status, and the students went out of their way to teach me how to dance the local Funk Rio!

Another meaningful *Exploring CQ* event occurred at the NUIF youth centre in Greenland, where I was conducting music workshops with a group of young Inuit. We performed a special concert for the community combining the Tamil and Greenlandic languages. I was introduced to the art of Katajjaq (Inuit throat singing) and the students made sure I ate whale, seal, and reindeer too!

When partnering with the Lahainaluna High School in Maui, I was able to share CQ workshops with students and create a music video with them which celebrated the school's diversity. The music video we made was a song on how to say thank you in Tongan, Marshallese, Tagalog, Hawaiian, and other languages that represented the students in the school. While there were cross-cultural challenges to overcome, in the end, the students felt a sense of recognition when they heard their language and owned this song that spread both CQ and 'aloha' – the beautiful Hawaiian concept that captures a sense of love, affection, peace, compassion, and mercy!

Thank You: Wilbur Sargunaraj [Feat: Lahainaluna High School Students]

Wilbur Sargunaraj
43.1K subscribers   Subscribe   👍 74   👎   ↪ Share   ...

Using the four capabilities of CQ, let's summarize again how you can develop cross-cultural relationships, at home or abroad. Ask yourself the questions below:

CQ DRIVE: What motivates you to actively engage in cross-cultural relationships? Can you think of specific challenges that might arise in these relationships, and how would you approach resolving them?

CQ KNOWLEDGE: What are some key cultural differences and similarities you believe could impact your interactions in cross-cultural situations? Reflect on an instance from your past where you faced a significant cultural difference. How did you deal with it?

CQ STRATEGY: Could you outline a detailed plan you would use to navigate through cross-cultural relationships? How would you adapt this plan based on the specific cultural subtleties you encounter?

CQ ACTION: Can you provide examples of specific behaviors or strategies you've used in the past to adapt to different cultural contexts? What mistakes did you make and what did you learn from them?

Some people have high CQ **Knowledge,** spouting facts about countries, but can lack the **drive** to develop relationships. Others can analyze cross-cultural situations and have a **strategy** of what should be done, yet find it difficult to take **action** and adapt in their interactions. It is important to develop all four of the capabilities to have high CQ and build meaningful cross-cultural relationships.

As you can see from the stories I have shared in this book, cultural intelligence can help us navigate cross-cultural challenges – such as bathing naked in a Japanese onsen, using an Indian squat toilet with no toilet paper, or being offered horse organs for dinner in Mongolia! While exercising CQ can help us with these situations, I hope you have also seen the great importance of CQ in developing meaningful relationships across cultures.

This leads me to the question. Who is your 'other'?

The takeaway of this book hinges on this question, because if you can confront your hidden bias, you will be able to start making deeper connections with people. Who knows? Maybe you will gain a new perspective, or share a meal, or even build a genuine friendship!

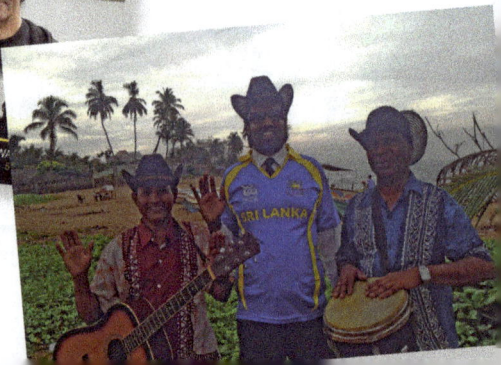

FROM TOLERANCE TO TRANSFORMATION

Many organizations use buzzwords like 'diversity and inclusion', they conduct workshops, programs, and even dedicate whole departments to these ideas. Yet, if there isn't a desire for people to be connected in meaningful relationships, then these efforts will at best end with tolerance.

In countries that are defined by multiculturalism, I can see why the idea of tolerance is popular. We do need to get along with all of our differences, and tolerance may help us to a certain degree, but tolerance – denoting simply 'putting up with someone' – isn't enough for what we need.

People sometimes take this approach when it comes to encountering diversity. You stay on your side, I'll stay on mine, and we will tolerate each other. This is better than intolerance, but it doesn't help us to move forwards. Breaking barriers and being genuinely welcoming and inclusive, requires a radical transformation of our hearts to confront bias and develop meaningful relationships.

The Nature of Prejudice, published in the 1954 by Gordon Allport, suggests that prejudice and conflict can be reduced when members of different groups and cultures interact with each other. As positive interactions increase, deeper relationships can be formed as people become willing to confront the biases that they've held.

Simply being multicultural, attending folk festivals, eating food from different cultures, and celebrating that your country has a diverse population is not enough. Hiring people from a wide range of diverse cultures and backgrounds just to tick the diversity and inclusion box is not enough! These are just first steps on the journey to move beyond tolerance. What is required is a transformation of hearts where people of diverse backgrounds are welcomed, where they can belong, and where they can be equal.

CHECK YOUR PRIVILEGE

Confronting racism, prejudice and discrimination starts when we realize that we may have advantages because of where we are born, our skin colour, our accent, our gender and other factors. This is not about making yourself feel guilty, but instead it's about opposing systemic and institutional racism by realizing that we have privilege, while others may be oppressed and disadvantaged. While it can be uncomfortable, reflecting on our privilege and the oppression that others face is an important step to becoming culturally intelligent citizens who welcome and treat others equally.

A couple of final stories. The journey of moving beyond tolerance makes me think of an event that my Emirati friend and I organized in Dubai, in the United Arab Emirates a number of years ago. He shared his frustrations regarding how several of his friends in Dubai kept to their own cultural groups. He wanted to see more interaction happening outside work between expats and Emiratis, so we organized one of the first *Exploring CQ* cross-cultural events. Using social media, we invited people to an informal gathering by the Tolerance Bridge, which is an actual bridge in Dubai named after the International Day of Tolerance! Our goal was to create a safe space where people could start meeting with each other and having positive interactions. It might sound simplistic, but for many Emiratis and expats, this was the first time they were getting to know each other on a personal level. We enjoyed a wonderful evening of sharing stories, listening to each other, asking questions, and of course sharing delicious food.

Another *Exploring CQ* event that stands out to me was with the Ngāti Awa Iwi (tribe) in Aotearoa, New Zealand. I was invited by Tohunga (elder) Dr. Pouroto Ngaropō to the Iramoko Marae (traditional Māori meeting house) where I was able to deepen my understanding of Māori culture and what the community is doing to build relationships between Māori and New Zealanders. We collaborated on creating a music video for a song I had written titled "Whanaungatanga", which explores the Māori principle of interconnectedness. The song is a celebration of the Māori culture and my hope is that it will inspire people in Aotearoa and around the world to join with each other in Aroha (love). Bringing the *Exploring CQ* event to diverse communities has been incredibly fulfilling. It's an opportunity to learn from remarkable individuals who actively cultivate relationships, inspiring others within their circles to embark on the initial steps of engaging with their 'other'.

Thank you for reading this book! Increasing our cultural intelligence is so important – it helps us to move beyond tolerance and towards one another, to see other people as human beings, to move away from us-and-them mindsets. CQ prevents us from being afraid of differences as we become more open-minded and interested in learning from new encounters.

In the end, our hearts can be transformed as we learn to challenge our biases and enter into meaningful relationships with our perceived 'other'. These relationships enable our societies to become places where people are valued and loved. I am so glad you have taken this journey with me to increase your CQ!

EPILOGUE

The sun was going down as I arrived at the Al Quoz migrant workers camp in Dubai. I was here to play cricket, have a few conversations over chai, and film a few sequences for the feature film I was working on called *Simple Superstar* – a story about the value of every person.

The workers in the camp had left their families back home to work in the Middle East. As we brought out our gear, a few curious workers stopped by, and soon we had around 200 migrant workers surrounding us, very interested in what was going on. There were workers from Pakistan, Bangladesh, India, Nepal, Afghanistan and other countries. Some seemed skeptical about our presence, especially because there is not much mingling between the classes in Dubai, and this is especially the case with migrant workers who are segregated and marginalized.

Sadly, as I started to perform, I realized the small speaker and microphone that we had brought were malfunctioning! Performing with a useless microphone, I went around the tight circle we had formed and asked the workers to teach me a few phases in their language. There were eruptions of laughter as I did my best to learn phrases in Pashto, Nepali, and Urdu. Once the workers realized I was genuinely interested in entering into their world they really started to engage with me.

As we immersed ourselves in this cultural exchange, a huge migrant worker who looked like a bald Arnold Schwarzenegger stepped into the middle of the group. He didn't seem interested in what was going on and quickly put an end to our party by motioning me to come. He asked for my name and where I was from. I told him my name was Wilbur, and that I was from India. I asked him the same, and with his two hands raised above his head he shouted "Pakistan!" and all the Pakistani workers shouted "Zindabag" (which means 'long live').

My heart immediately sank! I was surrounded by patriotic Pakistanis and started thinking how I was going to navigate this situation! Was this man going to punch me, berate me or start yelling at me to get out of his neighbourhood?

He did nothing of the sort! Instead, he started asking me to teach him Tamil! I shared a few words with him and he taught me a few phases in Urdu. Once again the workers started to enjoy this unique cross-cultural exchange. Then, abruptly, he called for silence and in front of this diverse crowd and said something in English that I'll never forget.

"Wilbur, no one comes here to see us. You come here, you make us laugh and learn, you make us happy. You are the top guy buddy. You are all top!"

Before I had a chance to process what he was saying, he took my hand, raised it high up in the sky, and yelled out "India and Pakistan – we are friends! Not new friends! Old friends!"

At that moment all the migrant workers lifted their hands up as well and there were huge cheers that echoed around the Al Quoz neighbourhood! As the sun set and our CQ celebration came to an end, I realized that a group of migrant workers living in Dubai were teaching me a sacred lesson about what happens when people from all walks of life come together, bringing all their differences to celebrate their common humanity.

This moment will stay with me for the rest of my life. Something beautiful happens when we enter into the world of our 'other', and I hope you will discover this as you embark on your cultural intelligence journey!

INDIA

FEATURES   NEWS & UPDATES   REVIEWS +   PHOTOS   VIDEOS   FEATURED ARTIST   GIG CALENDAR

Home » Features » Get A First Look At Wilbur Sargunaraj's Debut Film This November

Get A First Look At Wilbur Sargunaraj's Debut Film This November

The YouTube star will reveal the trailer of his film 'Simple Superstar' and also perform tracks from the album by the same name in India

| *Features*   October 23, 2012

Tell us about your movie *Simple Superstar*? It's not Hollywood, Tollywood or Kollywood. This movie is definitely Wilburwood. This movie has been made by Wilbur fans. It's for the fans, by the fans... it's almost a movement in itself. Many people are climbing up the ladder but I wanted to climb down the ladder. Since this movie has been made by the common people, I wanted to show people how to climb down the ladder and celebrate the common man.

Where has the film been shot? The movie has been shot in Tamil Nadu, Mumbai and Dubai and basically with fans from 20 different countries who sent their footage. I wanted to involve my fan base and incorporate social media. It's the fun of living in the era of the Facebook and the Twitter.

Poster of Simple Superstar

TheNational

Wilbur Sargunaraj now in a movie!

By - TNN | Updated: Jan 15, 2013, 09:08 IST

YouTube star films in Dubai, thanks to army of fans
Martin Croucher
May 5, 2012

ABOUT THE AUTHOR

Wilbur Sargunaraj is a musician, speaker, and Cultural Intelligence Facilitator. His years of cross-cultural experience, combined with his genuine love for connecting with people from diverse backgrounds, have given him a unique voice in the field of CQ.

Wilbur has pioneered a series of interactive and ground-breaking CQ concert events, exhibitions and workshops. His focus is on helping individuals and organizations navigate today's multicultural complexities by sharing valuable knowledge and fascinating anecdotes from his journeys.

Wilbur has worked with organizations such as NPR, Airbus, IOM, Ottawa Tourism, Steps International and numerous international schools to develop cultural intelligence through workshops, music videos and campaigns. He is a recipient of the Queen Elizabeth II Platinum Jubilee medal for his contributions in the field of education.

Wilbur's mission is to make the 'common' extraordinary. He has published a children's book titled *How to be a Simple Superstar* and has launched several collaborative musical projects. He actively supports the Ponnagam Destitute Center, which was founded by his parents.

Wilbur was born in a small prairie town on Treaty 7 Territory, Alberta, Canada; grew up in sweltering Tamil Nadu, India; and now resides in the freezing Canadian Prairies. He is an aviation enthusiast and contributes articles to UK-based Airliner World magazine. Wilbur is a cricket lover, aurora borealis hunter, chicken 65 eater and cardamom tea drinker!

Wilbur Spreads His Comedic Gospel of Love

An Interview arranges his Jakarta with his Bollywood influences to two laugh out

"There's a kind sacred in Wilbur, like a 21st-century electronic protestants..."

Wilbur Sargunaraj: Man who makes common EXTRA-ORDINARY

the spur of the movement

FIRST CLASS SIR!

news & times
Maple Creek

Helping the world come together: Q & A with Wilbur Sargunaraj

Roger Ebert
Following

Wilbur Wants a Love Marriage. Dare you not to like this Indian music video with its smiling bride. http://j.mp/cpR9rX

56   33

8:14 PM · 27 Feb, 2011

BBC 🔒 Sign in   News   Sport   Weather
NEWS
Home   Video   World   Asia   UK   Business   Tech   Science
US & Canada

THE CANADA SONG
Courtesy Wilbur Sargunaraj

the love marriage

Spriha's Corner
Spriha Srivastava

Let's make the common extraordinary

He is witty, he is creative and by this music you laugh and dance at the same time. He is India's latest Youtube sensation Wilbur Sargunaraj. For all those of you who still haven't heard of him, it's high time you familiarise yourself with the growing craze of Wilbur Sargunaraj. And it's not tough. All you need to do is search for him in Youtube and you will see his unique videos by the name of 'Supercall' and his hit songs like 'Love Marriage' 'Chicken 65'...

...just his sense of humour and creativity but his songs touch a long way and become India's first and biggest Youtube star. An extremely humorous show to watch Mr. Wilbur in his element. Wilbur's music can touch your love and you will see yourself humming his songs non stop.

Everything about him is different, starting from his style, his songs, his feel and his music. The best part is he makes his videos so simple, introducing Wilbur I went for a show in London. I think...

He turns the common into the extraordinary

...ada's record-

Musician, performer, educator and a humanitarian Wilbur Sargunaraj has a huge fan base all over the world. His satirical videos has already been viewed by thousands and his 'supercall solution videos' like how to...

❝❞

My works, whether it is music or videos, it is all about giving the common people a voice. For example for the video of the album 'Love Marriage' I use now...

An enlightening cross-cultural experience with Exploring CQ

Humboldt

The Simple Superstar

If you don't know Wilbur, you are a waste!. BT catches up with the popular and super-talanous Wilbur Sargunaraj

METRO

meet Wilbur

Photo: Deepak Daniel

NANDRI AND THANK YOU!

Writing this book was harder than I thought! I had to take a break from various projects and devote a full year to work on *Exploring CQ*. The book would not have been possible if it wasn't for the help of a small and dedicated team of simple superstars!

LeeAnne Benjamin, your contributions and insightful perspectives have been so valuable in shaping this book. I have appreciated our discussions about culture and I am inspired by how you practically use CQ in your everyday life!

Dave Burton I would like to thank you for the time and skill you invested in editing this book! Working with my evolving writing skills is no small feat (and any misplaced commas are my doing, not yours)! Thank you for believing in this project!

Gord and Louise Adnams, thank you for taking this stranger into your house years ago and allowing me to be part of your family! You have not only invested in this book, but in my life, and I am forever grateful to you both! Thank you, mom Louise, for your valuable advice and inputs!

Tammy Willman thanks so much for believing in *Exploring CQ*, and for pushing me to write it. You are a wonderful friend and I am so inspired by your passion to develop meaningful relationships!

Anna Muthu Diederichs Akka! Thank you for the beautiful design work throughout the book and for your assistance in creating the promotional material. I look forward to the day we can meet in person and share delicious dosai and filter coffee!

Cathy Barisow, thanks for your encouragement and feedback! Linda Thiessen thank you for your support and for allowing me to use your home as a writing retreat centre. Brother Jared 'DJ Deli' Funk: 'I have a friend'! I am so thankful for all the countless chinwags and movie nights. Eden Ebylin and Kaeson R. thanks for always keeping me grounded!

Valar Sivassoriyan – even though you are not here with us, I hope your amazing legacy will continue through this book. You enabled me to explore cultural intelligence and build relationships around the world. I miss you, my friend!

Appa thanks for all the sacrifices you and Amma made in order that I can be who I am today! We may not always see eye-to-eye, or share the same cultural values all the time, but I know your love for me has no bounds! I am so thankful for all the great times we have shared watching cricket together! Especially the India vs. Pakistan matches!

I am forever thankful to my friends near and far who have helped increase my cultural intelligence!

Above all thanks to the Creator who shows us how to build bridges of love!

Soli Deo Gloria

EXPLORE FURTHER!

For bookings, information, and
additional resources visit:

www.wilbur.asia

Instagram, Tik Tok and X   @wilburworldwide

Wilbur World Wide YouTube Channel

The *Exploring CQ* Exhibition

The CQ Chats Podcast

Music available on iTunes, Spotify and all digital streaming platforms

Also available from Wilbur Sargunaraj *How to be a Simple Superstar.* A child's guide to becoming the best version of themselves!

Wilbur's Lungi Pants

EXPLORING CQ

How do I build bridges with my "other"?

How can I work towards genuine reconciliation?

What is preventing me from making friends with people from different cultures?

How do I overcome my fear of what is different?

www.ingramcontent.com/pod-product-compliance
Lightning Source LLC
Chambersburg PA
CBHW070108030426
42335CB00016B/2068